THE QUEST

Finding Faith That Calms the Storms of Life

THE QUEST

Finding Faith That Calms the
Storms of Life

HENSLEY
PUBLISHING

ISBN 1-56322-078-4

The Quest

I dedicate this study to every believer who has a burning desire to rise above the struggles with your own human frailties. May each of you find that joyful place in Jesus Christ where every thought and purpose and relationship in your life is under the loving control of the Holy Spirit.

DOROTHY HELLSTERN

How to use this program for a small group study

The most effective way to use this Bible study is in a small group of 10 to 15 believers who are all sincerely seeking to grow spiritually. It should be led by someone who is also on this quest. To complete the program, your group will need to meet weekly for 10 to 12 weeks. Each member should have his own copy of The Quest and his own Bible. Look for leader's helps in the back of this book.

How to use this program on your own

If you prefer to complete this program at your own pace, it is quite possible to do so. It may be what you need to help you grow stronger spiritually or if you're looking for a fresh approach to personal Bible study. Simply follow the procedure for each study. Read the text material and give as much time as you need to the Bible studies. Then respond to the questions. Look for suggested responses in the back of this book. You may want to check these after you write your own. Be sure to respond to the **THINK ABOUT IT** questions.

Preface

When I began gathering this material and organizing it, I was doing it for my personal use. It's actually the culmination of some serious personal Bible study and many years of trying to learn how to walk in the light of the truths I found there. These truths are infinitely more useful to me than something merely nice to know. They're divine "life" in every sense of that word. Indeed, they've become like an anchor for my soul and spirit. I will be eternally grateful to the Holy Spirit, my Teacher and my Guide, for helping me establish these powerful truths in my heart.

As I prepared this material for myself, I began to realize that there might be others who would appreciate this simple, succinct presentation of some of the basic precepts of the Christian faith. I confirmed this when I used it in a weekly Bible study. Those who attended agreed that it had, indeed, strengthened their faith in God and their commitment to read and believe and live by His Word.
If you're a new believer, you may find answers here for some of the same questions I've asked. If you're a believer of long standing, you may find in this program a fresh approach to Bible study, and reinforcement for what you already know. It is my prayer that this study will help you to experience a closer relationship with your Heavenly Father as the Holy Spirit develops in you the nature of the Son.

Table of Contents

Introductory Session   *Page*

Unit 1   Who Is God to Me?

Day 1   What Is God Like?...17

Day 2   What Is Man Like?..19

Day 3   How Does God Want to Relate to Us?..21

Day 4   How Does God Want Us to Relate to Him?..23

Day 5   How Does God Want Us to Relate to Other People?............................25

Unit 2   What Was Jesus' Mission?

Day 1   Who Was Jesus Christ?...27

Day 2   Why Did He Come to Earth?..29

Day 3   Why Was the Virgin Birth Necessary?...31

Day 4   Why Was a Sinless Life Necessary?...33

Day 5   Why Was Calvary Necessary?..35

Unit 3   What Was Jesus' Triumph?

Day 1   What Does His Resurrection Mean to Us?...37

Day 2   How Does His Triumph Help the Sinner?...39

Day 3   What Does the Blood Covenant Mean to Us?......................................41

Day 4   Where Is Jesus Now?...43

Day 5   Where Do We Fit in God's Agenda?..45

Unit 4   Who Is the Holy Spirit to Me?

Day 1   Why Did the Holy Spirit Come?...47

Day 2   Why Is He Important to the Church?...49

Day 3   How Does He Help Us?...51

Day 4   How Do We Walk in the Spirit?..53

Day 5   How Do We Use the Spirit's Gifts?..55

Unit 5   What Is Not True Faith?

Day 1   Why Is Faith So Important?...55

Day 2   Faith Is Not Mental Assent or Acceptance of Physical Evidence.................59

Day 3   Faith Is Not Works or Special Abilities..61

Day 4   Faith Is Not Hope...63

Day 5   Faith Is Not a Feeling or a Magic Wand...65

Unit 6   **What Is True Faith?**

Day 1   Faith Is a Decision to Believe God..............................67

Day 2   Faith Is a Very Real Force..69

Day 3   Faith Is Life...71

Day 4   Faith Is a Gift from God...73

Day 5   Faith Is Trusting the Word of God.............................75

Unit 7   **How Do We Use Faith?**

Day 1   Remember Who Lives in Us.......................................77

Day 2   Focus on the Promises, Not the Problems................79

Day 3   Apply the Force of Faith with Words........................81

Day 4   Be Willing to Wait as Long as it Takes....................83

Day 5   Praise God for the Victory...85

Unit 8   **What Are the Enemies of Faith? Part I**

Day 1   Insufficient Bible Study..87

Day 2   Prayerlessness...89

Day 3   Pride and a Hardened Heart.......................................91

Day 4   Unforgiveness and Strife..93

Day 5   A Sense of Unworthiness...95

Unit 9   **What Are the Enemies of Faith? Part II**

Day 1   Double-Mindedness...97

Day 2   Greed and Covetousness...99

Day 3   Depending upon Religion or Tradition....................101

Day 4   Fear...103

Day 5   Wrong Confession...105

Unit 10   **Where Am I Now in My Spiritual Growth?**

Day 1   Who Is Ruling My Life?..107

Day 2   How Steadfast Am I in Times of Trial?..................109

Day 3   Do I Know How to Do Spiritual Warfare?.............111

Day 4   Is My Life a Model of Holiness?.............................113

Day 5   Am I Abiding in Christ?...115

Closing Session

Suggestions for Group Leaders

Introductory Session

There is, deep within each human heart, a yearning to KNOW that there is someone "out there" somewhere with answers to our nagging questions and solutions for the inevitable problems that arise in life. The Creator made us this way. He wants us to seek Him, for He alone can supply the truth for our questions and the blessings we need to solve our problems. Many souls have sought Him and found Him in His Word. And yet, for every one who is searching, there are countless others who continue to stumble through life, hoping for answers and solutions without ever knowing how to find them.

Without doubt, God wants us to know Him. His desire is for each of His children to become a witness to the world, expressing His love by the new nature (His nature) that is ours. If we're to fulfill His purpose for us, we must always be willing disciples, eager to learn all that He wants to reveal to us about Himself, about Jesus, and about our place in His Kingdom.

This study is a quest. Our goal will be to increase our knowledge and understanding of God's ways and purposes and how we fit into His agenda. We'll learn all we can about Jesus — what He has already done for us, what He wants to do for us now, and what He wants us to do for Him at this time in our life. What we learn will then become the basis for our faith, because knowing about God and His Son is not enough in itself. We must respond to what we learn. We must believe it, receive it into our spirit, and allow it to transform us from the inside. This quest is the key to growing spiritually, and that is the key to living a victorious life.

How to use the program with a leader and group meetings

The most effective way to use this program is in a small group of 10 to 15 believers who are all sincerely seeking to grow spiritually. It should be led by someone who is also on this quest. For greatest effectiveness, your group will need from 10 to 12 weeks to complete the program. Each member of the group should have his own copy of The Quest and his own Bible.

After this *Introductory Session*, each member of the group will spend about 45 minutes, preferably on a daily basis during the week, studying the five lessons in the unit. Then, the group will come together at an appointed time and place. The leader will guide the members in a discussion of the material you've studied during the week. You will talk about the concepts and go over your responses to the Bible studies. You should feel free, of course, to ask questions. Some of you will want to volunteer to share your thoughts about how you will apply what you've learned to your own personal experiences.

Depending upon the participants and the time allowed for the meeting, your group might want to have a time at the close of the meeting for sharing needs and praying for one another.

Determine to grow spiritually

If this program is to be successful for you and for other members of your group, you should commit to allowing sufficient time and doing whatever it takes to be an active, well-prepared participant. Here are some suggestions for doing that:

• Try to be present for each meeting. The concepts build upon each other from week to week, and your consistent attendance is important.

• Try to complete all five of the studies before each group meeting. Set aside a time each day during the week to do one study. Follow a regular procedure for each.

>—Pray before you begin and after you finish, declaring your desire to learn and grow. You may want to memorize and pray one of the foundation prayers from the Introduction.
>
>—Read the text material and give some serious thought to the concept.
>
>—The **KEY SCRIPTURES** (━●) are especially important. Be sure to read them as you study.
>
>—Read the scriptures in **STUDY THE WORD** (📖) and write your response to each one. These will be discussed in the group meetings.
>
>—In **THINK ABOUT IT** (**?**), write about how you expect to apply what you've learned. This is for your personal use and will not be read by anyone else unless you choose to share your thoughts at the group meeting.

• Participate in the group discussions. Realize that every member is attending the class because of a desire to learn. A question you ask or something you contribute to the discussion may be what another member needs to hear at that time.

• Come to each study and to each group meeting with a receptive spirit. God may be able to speak to you through a scripture or through what someone else has to say. This word from God could have a strong impact upon your life.

OUR SCRIPTURE FOUNDATION (What God wants to say to us)

It is essential for us, as born-again believers, to accept the Word of God as final authority in all questions that pertain to spiritual matters. Therefore, from the beginning and throughout this study, our quest will always be based on the following scriptures. They tell us plainly what God says about what He wants us to know and to become with His help. Emphasis in all scriptures is added by the author.

> *This is life eternal, that they might KNOW thee the only true God, and Jesus Christ, whom thou hast sent. (Jn. 17:3 KJV)*

> *Why is it that he gives us these special abilities to do certain things best? It is that God's people will be equipped to do better work for him, building up the Church, the body of Christ, to a position of strength and maturity; until finally we all believe alike about our salvation and about our Savior, God's Son, and all BECOME FULL-GROWN in the Lord — yes, to the point of being FILLED FULL with Christ. (Eph. 4:12-13 TLB)*

> *Long to GROW UP into the fullness of your salvation; cry for this as a baby cries for his milk. (1 Pet. 2:3 TLB)*

> *If you continue in my word, you are truly my disciples, and you will KNOW the truth, and the truth will make you free. (Jn. 8:31-32 RSV)*

> *Grace and peace be yours in abundance through the KNOWLEDGE of God and of Jesus our Lord. His divine power has given us everything we need for life and godliness through our KNOWLEDGE of him who called us by his own glory and goodness.... For this very reason, make every effort to add to your faith goodness; and to goodness, KNOWLEDGE.... (2 Pet. 1:2-5 NIV)*

OUR PRAYER FOUNDATION (What we want to say to God)

Since God's intense desire is for us to KNOW Him, He provides every means possible by which we may learn what He wants us to know. We have His written Word, and we have the powerful Holy Spirit as our Teacher. However, God never forces His children to seek knowledge of Him or to ask help of the Holy Spirit. He leaves this choice entirely to us.

UNDERSTANDING THE TERMS

seek: to inquire for or request earnestly.

final authority: a source of influence which is accepted above all others as the standard for life and conduct and is not subject to debate or question.

foundation: the base that gives support to whatever is built upon it.

full-grown: describes those whose senses are trained by practice to discriminate between what is good and noble and what is evil and contrary to divine or human Law. (Heb. 5:25 AMP)

mature manhood: nothing less than the standard height of Christ's own perfection; (Eph. 4:13 AMP)

When, deep within our spirit, there comes a yearning to know Him and to please Him, then we will instinctively realize that we cannot pursue the quest with our own intellect or our own effort alone. We must cry out to Him and declare our desire and our need for the Holy Spirit to reveal the truths of God's Word to us. Throughout the Bible we find prayers of others who have done the same and have received the help they sought. Their prayers can be our request, too, for this is what God wants to hear from His children. Here are several of those prayers, adapted to make them our own.

From Moses:

> *Now, therefore, I pray thee, if I have found favor in thy sight, show me now thy ways, that I may KNOW thee and find favor in thy sight.*
> *(Ex. 33:13 RSV)*

From David:

> *Make me to KNOW thy ways, O LORD; teach me thy paths. Lead me in thy truth and teach me, for thou art the God of my salvation; for thee I wait all the day long. (Ps. 25:4-5 RSV)*

From Solomon:

> *Heavenly Father, I receive your words and treasure up your commandments, making my ear attentive to skillful and godly Wisdom, and inclining and directing my heart and mind to understanding, applying all my powers to the quest for it. (from Prov. 2:1-2 AMP)*

From Paul:

> *I pray to you, the glorious Father of my Lord Jesus Christ, to give me wisdom to see clearly and really understand who Christ is and all that he has done for me. I pray that my heart will be flooded with light so that I can see something of the future he has called me to share. (Eph. 1:17-18 TLB)*

Your personal goals for this program:

What do you see as the weakest areas of your spiritual life?

_____

_____

_____

_____

_____

Write what you want this Bible study to do for you.

_____

_____

_____

_____

List specific steps you will take to assure that you can and will reach your goals.

_____

_____

_____

_____

_____

How Does God Want to Relate to Us?
DAY 3

Love is the truth behind all other truths. Love prompted the Creator to form the universe and put man in it. He IS love, and to satisfy love, there must be a recipient with a kindred spirit. God's love is a strong force, capable of melting the hardest, coldest heart and even changing nations.

God loves each of His children on the basis of the relationship, not on the basis of performance. He loves a "good" child with no greater love than a "bad" child. God's love cannot be bought, forced, or earned; it is not the product of even the most diligent effort. God is light, and all light in the universe originates from Him and gives life to all it touches. Just so, God is love, the source of all love, and this love is as vital to our well being as light or air. Because God understands this need far more than we ever will, His love is always present, always offered, and always life-giving. God's kind of love does not originate in the hearts, minds, and souls of other human beings. It comes forth from the very heart of the Creator.

We live in a sin-warped world. Every human being and every part of Creation was affected by Adam's sin. With Satan in control, all the miseries associated with sin make life on earth anything but the paradise God intended it to be. Throughout the ages, Satan has effectively deceived people into thinking that God brought on all their suffering. Nothing could be further from the truth. All of God's dealings with mankind have been motivated by His love for us. His great desire is to help us live free from the bondage of sin and its consequences. He has always wanted to make it possible for us to live in unbroken fellowship with Him. The world needs to know this.

God's purpose for the Old Covenant was to provide for His people what they could not provide for themselves through what the sinful world offered. Every ritual and every commandment was for their benefit, to protect them from spiritual, mental, and physical forces beyond their ability to comprehend or control. These forces separated them from God, robbed them of peace, and brought sickness and disease.

As the ultimate expression of His love for us, God sent His Son to pay the penalty for our sins and to usher in a New Covenant, sealed in His own blood. With Satan's power broken, we can be reconciled to God and restored to our

KEY SCRIPTURE

In this was manifested the love of God toward us, because that God sent his only begotten Son into the world, that we might live through him. Herein is love, not that we loved God, but that he loved us…Hereby know we that we dwell in him, and he in us, because he hath given us of his Spirit.
(1 Jn. 4:9, 13 KJV)

rightful place in His family. We now have a way to live IN the world without being OF the world. He showed His love even further by sending the Holy Spirit to reveal the truth to us. He empowers us to do what we could never do in our human weakness; that is, to carry out God's plan of taking His love to the world.

God's Word makes it abundantly clear that He wants to have a close, intimate relationship with each of us. Our spiritual growth depends upon our understanding this about God, and upon our willingness to seek Him. If we "draw nigh to God, He will draw nigh to us."

📖 **STUDY THE WORD**

Read the five short chapters of 1 John. Explain why you think this little book is often called God's "Love Letter to Believers."

_____

_____

_____

_____

_____

Read John 4:1-26. This is the story of the woman at the well. Explain how, by speaking to her at all, Jesus demonstrated that the Father's love transcends … social prejudice.

_____

… age-old racial hatreds.

_____

… the most blatant sin.

_____

I have loved you with an everlasting love.
(Jer. 31:3)

? **THINK ABOUT IT**

How has this study changed your view of some situation in your own life?

_____

_____

_____

_____

How Does God Want Us to Relate to Him?
DAY 4

The key to receiving God's love is not a secret, nor is it complex. Jesus taught it to His followers as the two Great Commandments, and He lived His entire life on earth in obedience to them. The old Law and its many demands are no longer binding to us. He requires of us only two things: love God and love one another. These commandments are, of course, for OUR benefit, because obedience to them is the surest way to experience the love, joy, and peace that He wants us to have while we walk in this world.

The most significant term in these commandments, and, perhaps, the one we most often overlook, is the word "all." This means far more than a passing nod in His direction now and then. It means complete submission to Him. If we seek Him with ALL our heart, we have his promise that our needs will be met. If we love Him with ALL our mind, we'll study His Word and meditate on His thoughts day and night and will succeed in all we undertake (Ps. 1:3). If we love Him with ALL our soul, we'll direct our devotion toward Him so fully and completely that our will and our emotions will be under His control. His love and compassion and joy will become OUR love and compassion and joy. If we love Him with ALL our strength, we will lay at His feet our very life and allow Him to "quicken" us with His life-giving strength.

Our soul gives expression to what is in our spirit. Therefore, when our spirit is in vital relationship with God, we will experience love flowing into us from the Source of love — genuine, life-giving, life-changing, healing, powerful, victorious love. The doorway to heaven, then, is whole-hearted acknowledgement of God's love for us and our love for God. This must be the great quest of life. By deliberate choice, we give Him all that we have — our heart, our intellect, our emotions, our possessions, our time, and our relationships. We acknowledge Him and express our love and gratitude to Him in praise and worship.

Most of us tend to think of the relationships in our lives as separate and distinct compartments with OURSELF in the center. There's a compartment for our relationship with a spouse, other compartments for siblings, children and grandchildren, in-laws and relatives, friends, neighbors, and colleagues. Then, in a separate compartment, we have our relationship with God. This is not the way God wants it to be, for our relationship with Him affects all other

KEY SCRIPTURE

Jesus said unto him, Thou shalt love the Lord thy God with all thy heart, and with all thy soul, and with all thy mind. This is the first and great commandment. And the second is like unto it, Thou shalt love thy neighbor as thyself. On these two commandments hang all the law and the prophets (Mt. 22:37-40 KJV)

And he answering said, Thou shalt love the Lord thy God with all thy heart, and with all thy soul, and with all thy strength, and with all thy mind; and thy neighbour as thyself. (Lk. 10:27 KJV)

He will cleanse your hearts and the hearts of your children and of your children's children so that you will love the Lord your God with all your hearts and souls, and Israel shall come alive again (Dt. 30:6 TLB)

relationships, and it determines our physical, mental, and spiritual well-being. He doesn't want to be one PART of our life. He wants to BE our life. This requires from us a total surrender, but He will not force us into this position.

Some of the strongest characters in the Bible understood this principle. They knew they were merely "containers" of the Spirit of God. The Apostle Paul called himself an "earthen vessel." Even Jesus said that it was not He who did the works, but His Father. As we grow spiritually, we will realize that we're actually loving God more and surrendering more of our life to Him.

📖 **Study the Word**

Study Colossians 1:9-10. In this prayer, Paul reveals his concern for believers. What is it that he wants for them?

_____

Study John 17:17-26. In this prayer that Jesus prayed in the Upper Room on the night before He was crucified, what did Jesus ask? For what purpose?

_____

_____

Study Jeremiah 9:23-24. In this scripture, the writer tells us the things about which we are NOT to boast. What are they?

_____

_____

Then he tells us that we SHOULD boast about this. What is it?

_____

? **Think about it.**

What have you learned from this study that will help you develop a more personal relationship with God?

_____

_____

Write something specific that you plan to do to strengthen your relationship with God.

_____

Understanding the Terms

fellowship: one or more persons enjoying a time of being together and sharing similar interests and experiences.

communion: intimate exchange of thoughts and feelings.

follow: to wholeheartedly accept the guidance and teaching of a revered leader.

serve: to give honor and obedience to a Supreme Being. This means far more than merely "working for" God like a hired servant. We serve by allowing Him to work through us and out of gratitude and adoration, not duty.

commandment: an order, direction, or law issued by someone in a position of authority, to be obeyed without debate and without compromise.

Lord, take ALL of me.

Why Did He Come to Earth?
DAY 2

Most believers have heard the accounts of Jesus' birth, His miracles, His crucifixion, and His resurrection. Few, however, have a meaningful understanding of the purpose behind His coming to earth and what He was expected to accomplish while He was here. Knowing this is basic to knowing Jesus.

In order to understand why Jesus came to earth, we must first understand the legal impact of what took place in the Garden of Eden. (Gen. 3) Man was originally made for authority. He was to be ruler of the earth, its life, and its resources. (Ps. 8) Laws govern the entire universe, and any law works every time it's applied, unless a higher law is applied that supersedes it. The law of gravity, for example, is a very real, though unseen, physical law. We know that if we throw something into the air, it will fall toward the earth. However, there are other physical laws that enable birds and airplanes to fly and space craft to orbit the earth. There are also unseen spiritual laws that are just as real. God's grant of authority was a LEGAL matter, and Adam received it as his responsibility.

Satan's temptation to Adam and Eve was to the soul of man — his mind, his will, and his emotions. Satan was saying, "Look out for yourself. Get control and power. Then you'll be as God." This, of course, was a blatant deception, because Adam already had control and power under the authority of God. When he rebelled against God, he lost his right to rule. Since Satan now had legal authority to rule over man and the earth, Adam became Satan's slave. At that moment, the earth and all life on the earth, including human beings and every part of nature, came under the dominion of Satan and his demonic hosts, bringing about terrible consequences.

God could not, by His own spiritual laws, step in and repossess man's authority for him. God had to make a way to redeem fallen man and recover his lost authority without violating His own laws of justice. Angels could not do it, because they had never had legal rights to the earth or any part of creation. Only a member of Adam's race could take Adam's lost heritage and dominion from Satan. It had been given to man, lost by man, and, legally, man must recover it. But what man? As slaves of Satan, all of Adam's descendants were disqualified.

KEY SCRIPTURE
God said, Let Us [Father, Son, and Holy Spirit] make mankind in Our image, after Our likeness, and let them have complete authority over the fish of the sea, the birds of the air, the [tame] beasts, and over all of the earth, and over every thing that creeps upon the earth.
(Gen. 1:26 AMP)

To Adam, God said, "Because you listened to your wife and ate the fruit when I told you not to, I have placed a curse upon the soil. All your life you will struggle to extract a living from it. It will grow thorns and thistles for you, and you shall eat its grasses. All your life you will sweat to master it, until your dying day. Then you will return to the ground from which you came. For you were made from the ground, and to the ground you will return."
(Gen. 1:17-19 TLB)

A member of the human race was needed, but it had to be one upon whom Satan had no legal claim.

Jesus came to earth,

- to be the required sacrifice, the perfect Lamb, to atone for the sins of all mankind,
- to destroy the works of Satan,
- to redeem us from every form of the curse that is the penalty of sin, and
- to reconcile us to the Father and make it possible for us to be His children.

📖 STUDY THE WORD

Read Romans 5:1-21. Describe the contrast between what Adam did and what Jesus did.

_____

_____

_____

Read Colossians 1:9-23. How did Paul explain Jesus' purpose for coming to earth?

_____

_____

_____

_____

Read Romans 8:18-23. What will happen to creation at the time of our final redemption?

_____

_____

_____

Call His name Immanuel — God with us.
(Isa. 7:14)

❓ THINK ABOUT IT

How has this study changed the way you think about Jesus' coming?

_____

_____

_____

Why Was the Virgin Birth Necessary?
DAY 3

Man has always had difficulty accepting as truth what he cannot understand and explain with his intellect. We cannot see into the realm of the spirit or experience it with our human senses. The miracles of the Bible are often scorned by religious leaders and scholars who attempt to explain them away or somehow make them fit into the knowledge we already have. Through the work of dedicated archaeologists and scientists, more and more information is coming forth to confirm the biblical record. And yet, it's virtually impossible to explain to the mind of man what the Holy Spirit must reveal to his spirit. In fact, this is one of the main functions of this powerful gift that was promised to every one who would believe the Gospel message and receive salvation through Jesus Christ. The Holy Spirit is sent to "guide us into all truth."

Of all the miracles recorded in God's Word, the Virgin Birth would probably have to be listed as one of the most controversial. Scholarly theologians can give some seemingly persuasive reasons that the Virgin Birth was either impossible, improbable, or unnecessary. For the true believer, however, it is one of the most vital truths in all of scripture.

God went to great lengths to prepare the way for the coming of His Son and to inspire Old Testament writers to record every phase of the preparation. Centuries before the event, prophets announced details of His birth, for it had to be so unique and so miraculous that there could be no doubt that it was of God.

In his annunciation to Mary, the angel Gabriel said that the Holy Spirit would overshadow her, and she would bear a son. The great difference between this Child and any other human child was that no human father would pass on to Him the sin nature of Adam which had always been the curse of the human race. If Joseph had been His father, Jesus would have been Adam's descendant and Satan's slave, like everyone else. Thus, he would not be qualified to challenge Satan's authority. He had to be authentically human but not a descendant of Adam. Since Jesus was conceived by the Holy Spirit, He was NOT a fallen son of Adam, and Satan had no claim upon Him. And yet, He entered the world as all human beings do, "made of woman." As an authentic human being, then, He was legally qualified to reclaim what Adam had lost. The Virgin Birth was ABSOLUTELY NECESSARY to God's plan to redeem mankind.

KEY SCRIPTURE

Therefore the Lord himself shall give you a sign; Behold, a virgin shall conceive, and bear a son, and shall call his name Immanuel.
(Isa. 7:14 KJV)

Behold, a virgin shall be with child, and shall bring forth a son, and they shall call his name Emmanuel, which being interpreted is, God with us.
(Mt. 1:23 KJV)

We must accept this by faith, in the same way we must accept every great act of God and every spiritual truth,. It is essential for us to believe the truth and accuracy of every part of it, regardless of how "impossible" some of it may seem to be. The Virgin Birth is no exception. The truth of the Virgin Birth cannot be disputed apart from denying the divine inspiration and accuracy of the Word of God. To doubt it is to doubt everything else Jesus said and did. To doubt it is to doubt that Jesus could and did pay the penalty for our sins. To doubt that is to doubt our redemption and, subsequently, our hope for eternal life.

📖 **STUDY THE WORD**

Read Matthew 1:18-25. Matthew gave this account of the birth of Jesus after first tracing His genealogy. Why did Matthew think Jesus' genealogy was important to believers — especially Jewish believers?

_____

_____

_____

_____

Read Luke 1:26-38. This is the account of Gabriel's annunciation to Mary. What information did he give her that would help reassure her and confirm that her miracle was from God?

_____

_____

_____

Read Isaiah 7:10-14. The Holy Spirit spoke this prophecy through Isaiah. What evidence do we have that it was fulfilled?

_____

_____

_____

_____

For unto us a child is born.
(Isa. 9:6)

? **THINK ABOUT IT**

What have you learned in this study that you could share with someone who still has doubts about the accounts of the Virgin Birth?

_____

_____

_____

UNIT 3 What Was Jesus' Triumph?

What Does His Resurrection Mean to Us?
DAY 1

When the claims of justice had been met, Jesus was "vindicated by the spirit" and was "made alive by the spirit." (1 Tim. 3:16; I Pet. 3:18 NIV) As long as He was identified with sin, He was in the hands of Satan. Then, when He was judged and declared righteous in the eyes of the Supreme Judge of the universe, Satan no longer had a legal right to His body, mind, soul or spirit. When, as a human man, He had completely disarmed and dethroned Satan, Jesus came forth from the region of the dead. "He spoiled principalities and powers and made a show of them openly, triumphing over them in it." (Col. 2:15) Although death did its utmost to keep him bound, Jesus took the keys of death and hell. (Rev. 1:18) As Peter told the crowd that had gathered on the Day of Pentecost, "it was impossible for death to keep its hold on him." (Act. 2:23-24)

KEY SCRIPTURE

This man was handed over to you by God's set purpose and foreknowledge; and you, with the help of wicked men, put him to death by nailing him to the cross. But God raised Him from the dead, freeing him from the agony of death, because it was impossible for death to keep its hold on him.

(Acts 2:23-24 NIV)

When Jesus came out of the grave, He left ALL the miseries associated with sin behind Him. He had been punished for every sin of every human being in every age. Every debt had been paid in full, but He did not suffer those torments for sins He had committed. He willingly suffered what we deserved. Nothing we have ever done, no matter how noble or good, could hope to pay for even one of our sins. That Jesus paid our debt is a wonderful truth to know, and it's available to everyone who will choose to believe it and accept it. Instead of an eternity in hell, we can look forward to our own resurrection and eternal life in heaven. Indeed, we will need eternity to praise Him for His "amazing grace."

While hope for eternal life is vitally important, every believer must also understand the truth about what this has done for us here and now. Although it may be difficult for our minds to grasp, in the eyes of God, when Jesus died, vicariously we were IN Him. When He was buried, we were buried WITH Him. Every sin we have ever committed or will ever commit was buried with Him. When He arose, we arose WITH Him. All our sins and all the miseries associated with our sins should have been left behind in the tomb. In Him, we are free to live in all the newness and fullness of life that is ours as children of the Most High God.

When we look around us at the lives of others or consider the problems we have in our own life, it is obvious that very few of us are living in this fullness of life.

And yet, Jesus said that's why He came, "that we might have life — abundant life."(Jn. 10:10) It was His mission, His reason for coming to earth. If this was what He wanted for us, then each of us should make it our quest to learn whatever we need to learn in order to have what belongs to us through His resurrection. We must ask the Holy Spirit to reveal this truth to our spirit and to teach us how to walk in it.

UNDERSTANDING THE TERMS
resurrection: brought to life after having died.

vicarious: performed (or endured) by one person substituting for another.

📖 **STUDY THE WORD**

Read Romans 6:1-12. Explain the significance of water baptism in the light of this scripture.

_____

_____

_____

Read 2 Corinthians 5:14-21. What does Paul give as another result of what Jesus did for us?

_____

_____

In Philippians 3:7-11, Paul speaks of knowing Jesus and the "power of His resurrection." What do you think he meant?

_____

_____

_____

? **THINK ABOUT IT**

How would you explain Jesus' resurrection to someone who had never heard about it or who is skeptical about it?

_____

_____

_____

What have you learned from this study that has given you a new perspective about the resurrection?

_____

_____

_____

It was impossible for death to hold Him.
(Acts 2:24)

How Does His Triumph Help the Sinner?
DAY 2

In the eyes of God, there are only two kinds of people on earth: the saved and the unsaved. All humanity was identified with Jesus in death, but only those who believe are identified with Him in His resurrection. From the Word of God, we know the destiny of those in each category. The saved will be with Him in His Kingdom for all eternity. The unsaved will be separated from God and will live an eternal death with all the other unsaved ones. Out of His intense love, God sent Jesus to make a way for every human soul, throughout the world and through all the ages, to be set free from sin and rescued from hell. Considering such prospects, why isn't every man, woman and child on earth already among the saved? Why must God still look down and see countless thousands — perhaps millions — who are still unsaved?

There are still many who have never heard about Jesus and the cross because no one has ever told them. Others have heard but are depending upon their own "goodness" to make a way for them into God's grace; they simply do not yet understand their desperate need for a Savior.

For some, leaving the religious doctrines and traditions of their ancestors may be unthinkable. For others, the prospects of inevitable persecution and suffering are too costly a price to pay for choosing Jesus and the salvation He offers. Many people reject salvation because they stubbornly refuse to repent of their sins and turn away form their sinful ways. Satan is successfully deceiving them into believing that the pleasures and power this world offers are more to be desired than a place in God's Kingdom.

God has conferred upon us the ultimate gift of a will. Each of us has absolute freedom to make choices, and we exercise this privilege many times every day. Because of this, God cannot choose salvation for anyone. Nor can he justly do anything to prevent even one soul from rejecting Jesus. He can and will, however, do everything possible to get the message of the Gospel to every soul. In His master plan, He has placed this responsibility in the hands of His Church. The Church is His Body on earth. It's made up of all the believers (the saved) throughout the world, from every conceivable walk of life or nationality. God has sent the Holy Spirit to empower us for witnessing, but He will not force us to share our faith with the lost.

KEY SCRIPTURE
I have been crucified with Christ; it is no longer I who live, but Christ who lives in me; and the life I now live in the flesh I live by faith in the Son of God, who loved me and gave himself for me.
(Gal. 2:20 RSV)

How does Jesus' triumph help sinners? It doesn't at all, unless they hear about it and have a chance to respond. If any of us who believe had even the slightest concept of the hopelessness of eternity apart from God, we would never again take lightly our responsibility to spread the Good News to every living soul.

📖 STUDY THE WORD

Read Colossians 1:9-23. According to Paul, what was Jesus' part in our salvation?

_____

_____

UNDERSTANDING THE TERMS

reconciliation: bringing into harmony again after having been separated by discord.

imputed: transferred from one person to another.

What is our part?

_____

_____

_____

Read 2 Corinthians 5:14-21 and Colossians 2:9-15. How could you use these scriptures to reassure someone who might have doubts about his salvation?

_____

_____

_____

_____

_____

_____

❓ THINK ABOUT IT

Record how this study has affected your view of missionary efforts?

_____

_____

_____

_____

When I was still a sinner, He loved me and gave Himself for me.

How has it affected your view of personal witnessing?

_____

_____

_____

What Does the Blood Covenant Mean to Us?
DAY 3

At the Last Supper with His disciples, Jesus said, "This is my body that is broken for you. This is my blood of the New Covenant that is poured out for many unto the remission of sins." (Mt. 26:28) These men had lived under the Old Covenant, but they probably did not understand the significance of a New Covenant until the Holy Spirit revealed it to them after the Day of Pentecost. Without such revelation, we cannot comprehend it either. Since God's Word has much to say about this covenant and the one it replaced, we need to know how it affects us. This concept is vital to our quest for spiritual strength.

We can trace the entire Plan of Redemption by following these two covenants. In fact, our scriptures are divided that way — Old Testament and New Testament. A "testament" is the same as a "covenant." Covenants have always been important. Even primitive people sealed covenants between tribes and nations, usually with the shedding of blood by both parties. A blood covenant was considered the most binding of all, for it could not be broken without serious consequences. We do not usually seal covenants with blood today, but we still make covenants and seal them with signatures.

The Old Covenant was made between God and Abraham. It was sealed with the blood of animals. After that, it was continued with the practice of circumcision. As long as Abraham's descendants kept this practice, the terms of the Covenant were in effect. All that Abraham had would belong to God, and God would provide all their needs and protect them from their enemies. Because God knew they would not always keep their part of the Covenant, He established the system of animal sacrifice. The blood of animals would "atone for" or "cover over" their sins.

That system continued until Jesus came. Because He met every requirement of the Old Covenant, He qualified to be the blood sacrifice needed to atone for the sins of the entire world. After the Old Covenant had been fulfilled, everything connected to it was set aside. When Jesus broke the bread and gave the cup of wine to His disciples at the Last Supper, He was issuing in a New Covenant. Before another day would pass, He would seal this covenant with His own blood.

Since Jesus became the sacrificial Lamb, animal sacrifices are no longer required. He didn't just cover over our sins; He washed them away completely,

KEY SCRIPTURE

This is My blood of the new covenant, which is shed for many for the remission of sins. (Mt. 26:28 NKJV)

For you know that it was not with perishable things such as silver or gold that you were redeemed from the empty way of life handed down to you from your forefathers, but with the precious blood of Christ, a lamb without blemish or defect. (1 Pet. 1:18-20 NIV)

leaving us justified before the throne of God. We have only to believe it and receive it. As believers, we are now living under a Blood Covenant. Along with the forgiveness of sins, we have a right to all the other benefits that are legally ours.

Every time we take Communion (the Lord's Supper), we are symbolically committing to our part of this Blood Covenant. We should always remember that we belong to Him. Under this Covenant, He has a blood-bought right to our life and everything we have or will ever have. We should also remember that every promise in God's Word, from Genesis to Revelation, is a promise to all believers. Those precious promises are His part of the New Covenant.

📖 STUDY THE WORD

Read Exodus 24:4-8. Explain why the ritual described here was important to the spiritual life of God's people.

_____

_____

Read Jeremiah 31:31-34. Jeremiah prophesied a new covenant. How did he say it would be different from the Old Covenant?

_____

_____

Read Hebrews 8:6-13. What scripture is quoted here? What does it say about the covenants?

_____

_____

? THINK ABOUT IT

How has this study of the two covenants affected your understanding about who you are?

I am redeemed by the blood of the Lamb.

_____

_____

_____

Relate how you think this new understanding will affect the way you live.

_____

_____

_____

Where Is Jesus Now?
DAY 4

Any quest for spiritual maturity must grow out of an intense desire to know Jesus. The closer we come to knowing Him, the more we realize that our quest is actually becoming a pursuit of HIM. All that we've learned about Him makes us hunger for more intimacy with Him. But where do we find Him? We've learned that He came to earth, died on the cross, was buried and rose again. We know that, after a time of reunion with His disciples and others, He ascended into heaven. His disciples saw Him rise into the clouds, and they heard Him say that He would come again.

If we're to know Jesus, it's important for us to understand where He is now and what He is doing in our behalf. His ministry did not end with His ascension. He's seated on His throne at the right hand of the Father in heaven, and He's still carrying on His duties as our High Priest.

Under the Old Covenant, the Hebrews could go to God only through priests, and their sins could be forgiven only through the work of the High Priest. The duty of the priests was to offer gifts and sacrifices to God in behalf of the people. The High Priest performed his most important task once a year on the Day of Atonement. After preparing himself carefully, he entered the Holy of Holies, taking with him the blood of a sacrificial animal. He sprinkled the blood on the Mercy Seat to cover his own sins of the past year and those of the people of Israel.

At the moment Jesus died on the cross, the thick, heavy veil surrounding the holy of holies in the temple was split from top to bottom. This was a mighty miracle, and it has great significance for us. It means that the way to the presence of God has been opened. After His resurrection, Jesus met Mary Magdalene in the garden and cautioned her, "Touch me not, for I am not yet ascended to My Father." (Jn. 20:5-18) Then He appeared before the Father, taking His own blood as a sacrifice to atone for the sins of mankind. He was carrying out His first duty as High Priest for all those who would confess Him as Lord and Savior.

Just before He ascended, Jesus declared that ALL authority in heaven and earth was now His. That means He, our merciful and faithful High Priest and Mediator of the New Covenant, is Lord over all. Under the Old Covenant, the people had to come to the High Priest with their petitions and their sacrifices

KEY SCRIPTURE

Therefore God exalted him to the highest place and gave him the name that is above every name, that at the name of Jesus every knee should bow, in heaven and on earth and under the earth, and every tongue confess that Jesus Christ is Lord, to the glory of God the Father.
(Phil. 2:9-10 NIV)

for worship. Under the New Covenant, we can enter personally into the Throne Room of our Heavenly Father at any time and offer our petitions. Jesus is there as our Advocate, interceding for us when we sin, telling the Father that our sins have been washed away in His blood. The only acceptable "gifts" we can bring with us are gratitude, praise, and commitment.

Jesus carried out another duty as High Priest when He commissioned His disciples (and the Church) to "Go into all the world and preach the Gospel in My name" (Mt. 28:18-20). The same commission is ours today, and we have all the authority of God Himself backing our efforts.

UNDERSTANDING THE TERMS

mediator: a person who acts as an agent for another person.

advocate: a person who pleads another's cause.

intercession: making a request in behalf of another.

Mercy Seat: the cover of the Ark of the Covenant. Representative of the Throne of God in heaven.

Holy of Holies: the innermost enclosure of the Temple, where God's presence dwelt.

📖 **STUDY THE WORD**

Read Hebrews 5:1-10. This compares Christ's priesthood to the Levitical priesthood. How does it show that Jesus is qualified for the office of High Priest?

_____

_____

_____

Read Hebrews 8:1-6. From this scripture, describe where Jesus is now and what He is doing.

_____

_____

_____

Read Matthew 28:16-20 and Mark 16:14-20. Summarize what Jesus was asking of His followers and what He was promising them.

_____

_____

❓ **THINK ABOUT IT**

How has this study changed your view about what Jesus is doing for you now?

_____

_____

_____

How has it changed your thinking about prayer?

_____

_____

His name is above every name.

Where Do We Fit in God's Agenda?
DAY 5

The disciples, now called Apostles, wasted no time in beginning to carry out the Great Commission. They witnessed with great boldness, and thousands responded to the Good News they preached. Each new believer became another strong witness, winning the lost one by one and family by family. The believers began to gather on the first day of each week to celebrate the day on which Christ was resurrected and to hear more from the Apostles about what He taught and what He wanted of believers. These followers of Christ were called "Christians," and this was the beginning of the Church. Gradually, for them, it replaced temple worship and Sabbath observances. The most significant change of all, however, was in their love for one another. As Jesus had said, "By this all men will know that your are my disciples, if you love one another." (Jn. 13:34 NIV)

The ultimate aim in all that God has ever done is to reveal Himself and His love to mankind. His great work in redemption is to reveal His Son IN US. He wants each believer's life to become a visible expression of the life of Jesus. It is not something we strive to do or struggle to attain. It is not like a coat that we put on, and it is not piously and proudly keeping a set of rules and regulations prescribed by religious leaders. When we accept Jesus as our personal Redeemer, He actually comes to live within us — invisible but so real. Little by little, day by day, through our actions and reactions in every relationship, SELF must move out (and eventually die). More and more of Jesus and all that He is must move in. This is where we fit into His agenda.

It's important for us to remember that maturing, in any sense of the word, is a process, not a once-and-for-all event. Each of us has a great deal to learn and experience before we can even hope to be as spiritually mature as God wants us to be. Since each of us is at a different place in the maturing process, we must be understanding and nonjudgmental about the level of maturity we discern in other Christians. Our attitude toward others is an indisputable indication of our own level of maturity.

God has a master plan, and He has a specific plan for each individual who is ever born. No one is here by accident; no one is insignificant. Regardless of what career we may choose for ourselves, we are an important part of God's plan to win the unsaved. Wherever we go and whatever we do, we must remember that we're "containers" of the very nature of God. Ultimately, by His grace, we

🔑 **KEY SCRIPTURE**

This is my prayer that your love may abound more and more in knowledge and depth of insight, so that you may be able to discern what is best and may be pure and blameless until the day of Christ, filled with the fruit of righteousness that comes through Jesus Christ — to the glory and praise of God. (Phil. 1:9-11 NIV)

So then, just as you received Christ Jesus as Lord, continue to live in him, rooted and built up in him, strengthened in the faith as you were taught, and overflowing with thankfulness (Col. 2:6-7 NIV)

Rather, speaking the truth in love, we are to grow up in every way into him who is the head, into Christ. ... Therefore, be imitators of God, as beloved children. And walk in love, as Christ loved us and gave himself up for us, a fragrant offering and sacrifice to God (Eph. 4:15; 5:1-2 RSV)

will become who God wants us to be — a reflection of Himself and "a fragrant offering" to the world around us. That's what growing up into the fullness of Christ is all about; that's what God wants to see — "Christ in us, the hope of glory." (Eph. 4:13; Col. 1:27)

📖 STUDY THE WORD

UNDERSTANDING THE TERMS
The Church: the collective body of believers.

The Bride of Christ: this is a figurative way of comparing the Church in its glorified state with the glorified Christ as her Bridegroom.

The Body of Christ: This is a figurative way of comparing the Church to the parts and functions of a human body.

Read Matthew. 19:16-22. How does this story of the rich young ruler illustrate the importance of our choices and priorities?

_____

_____

_____

Read 2 Corinthians 5. What does Paul say about how we're to live?

_____

_____

_____

Read Colossians 1:9-29. What does Paul tell us about God's purposes for us?

_____

_____

_____

Read Philippians 1:9-11. What does Paul tell these believers that they should be doing while they wait for Christ's return?

_____

_____

_____

Christ in us,
the hope of glory.
(Col. 1:27)

? THINK ABOUT IT

How has this study changed your view about what God expects of you?

_____

_____

_____

List some specific changes you plan to make in your lifestyle.

_____

_____

_____

UNIT 4 Who Is the Holy Spirit to Me?

Why Did the Holy Spirit Come?
DAY 1

Because of our spiritual nature, most people instinctively acknowledge the existence of God. Because of the preaching of the Word, great numbers of people acknowledge that Jesus is the Son of God. Few of us, however, could say with assurance that we understand who the Holy Spirit is, what He has done, and what He is doing. Since He is indispensable to our spiritual welfare, we must learn all we can about our relationship with Him before we go any further in our quest.

The Holy Spirit is a member of the Godhead. Finite minds have difficulty with concepts like the Trinity, or three-in-one, but it has great significance in the spiritual realm. We know from God's Word that the Holy Spirit has the same attributes as the Father and the Son, and He is of great importance as the One who carries out the Father's plans.

Under the Old Covenant, God sent the Holy Spirit to rest UPON certain chosen individuals for a certain purpose and for a certain amount of time. He was there to guide the Hebrew fathers and to anoint the priests for their tasks. He inspired the writers and the prophets to give us the Word of God. When Jesus came to earth, the Holy Spirit was involved in every phase of His life from His conception to His resurrection and ascension. After His baptism, Jesus announced publicly that He was anointed of God to preach and teach, to heal the sick, and to set captives free. Everything He did on earth was through the power of the Holy Spirit.

At the Last Supper, Jesus announced to His disciples that the Father was going to send the Holy Spirit, not just upon them for a given time, but to live IN them forever. Jesus explained that this would be far better for them, because the Holy Spirit would not be limited by time and space as He had been. Rather, the Holy Spirit could be with each individual believer all the time and anywhere. He would empower them to do everything Jesus had done — preach with boldness, teach with inspired words, heal the sick, raise the dead, cast out demons, perform signs and wonders, and be victorious over sin.

The Acts of the Apostles is an account of the fulfillment of that announcement. The Holy Spirit came on the Day of Pentecost with great manifestations of

KEY SCRIPTURE

I will pray the Father, and He will give you another Helper, that He may abide with you forever — the Spirit of truth, whom the world cannot receive, because it neither sees Him nor knows Him; but you know Him, for He dwells with you and will be in you....He will teach you all things, and bring to your remembrance all things that I said to you....
(Jn. 14:16-17, 26 NKJV)

power. Jesus' disciples and other followers, trembling with fear, had been praying and waiting for the promised gift from above. After they were filled with the Holy Spirit, they preached boldly on the streets of Jerusalem to the same crowd that had called for the crucifixion of Jesus a short time before. They could never have carried out the Great Commission and established the Church with their own human abilities. With the power of the Holy Spirit, however, they would "turn the world upside down" with the Gospel message. If the infilling of the Holy Spirit was essential to everything they did at the beginning, how much more essential it is for us today, for the unsaved world is still waiting to hear the Good News!

📖 STUDY THE WORD

Read Psalm 51:10-12. What did David ask of God in this prayer?

_____

_____

Read Luke 4:14-21. What was unusual about Jesus' announcement in the synagogue?

_____

_____

UNDERSTANDING THE TERMS
The Trinity and the Godhead: both mean the union of three deities existing in absolute unity, and yet uniquely distinct.

Read Acts 1:1-8; 2:1-4. Why did Jesus tell His followers to wait in Jerusalem? What happened there?

_____

_____

Read John 20:19-23. What unusual thing did Jesus do? What did He instruct His disciples to do?

_____

_____

*In the last days,
God says,
I will pour out
my Spirit
on all people.*
(Acts. 2:17)

❓ THINK ABOUT IT

How has this study affected your understanding of the Holy Spirit?

_____

_____

Tell how you think this new understanding will affect the way you live.

_____

_____

Why Is He Important to the Church?
DAY 2

As they watched Jesus ascend into heaven, His disciples must have experienced overwhelming fear and helplessness. He had just charged them with a task they knew they could never accomplish without having Jesus with them. Although He had promised to be with them always, they had no way of knowing how He could possibly do that. While they waited in Jerusalem for the "gift" from the Father, their minds must have been full of doubt and confusion.

Then the Holy Spirit came, and they knew at once that Jesus Himself had come and had filled each of them with His own Spirit. They would never be the same again. The Holy Spirit brought Old Testament prophecies to their minds and revealed to them how these prophecies had been fulfilled in Jesus. Spiritual truths that Jesus had taught them suddenly had meaning. All fear was gone, replaced by a new boldness that compelled them to "go and tell" everyone who would listen, regardless of the danger. The Holy Spirit transformed humble men and women into a powerful force for the Kingdom of God. It was these Spirit-filled Christians who established the Church, the Body of Christ, on earth. From that day, God's great Plan of Redemption was in the hands of the Church. The Holy Spirit raised up leaders and workers and gave them the spiritual gifts they would need to carry out this awesome responsibility.

Satan knew he was defeated at Calvary, but he must have thought this truth would never reach beyond Jerusalem and that generation. With the coming of the Holy Spirit and the establishment of the Church, the Good News of salvation in Christ had the potential of reaching around the world. Satan began an all-out campaign to stamp it out, but to no avail. Those early Christians endured unbelievable persecution and suffering. Instead of defeating them, however, this served to disperse them and their Gospel message into other nations, and caused the Church to grow strong. Without the comfort, counsel and help of the Holy Spirit, the Church could not have survived those early years. Our New Testament was their legacy to the Church of every generation that followed them, because it became the manual for "walking in the Spirit."

Jesus said the Holy Spirit would come as the Spirit of Truth, and His truth has been indispensable to the Church in its ongoing battle against Satan's deceptions. Great power is available to any group of believers when the Holy Spirit is working in the lives of its members and leaders. Perhaps this is why Satan has worked furiously to keep us from learning about the Holy Spirit and

KEY SCRIPTURE
Ye shall receive power, after that the Holy Ghost is come upon you: and ye shall be witnesses unto me both in Jerusalem, and in all Judaea, and in Samaria, and unto the uttermost part of the earth. (Acts 1:8 KJV)

acknowledging our desperate need of Him. The history of the Church is dark with periods when the Spirit of Truth was almost silenced, allowing false teachers to lead whole generations away from God. Without the Holy Spirit, it would be easy for us, even now, to fall into bondage to man-made doctrines and occult practices. We can praise God that the Holy Spirit is still at work in the Church today.

📖 Study the Word

UNDERSTANDING THE TERMS

edify: to build up or strengthen spiritually.

persecution: oppression inflicted upon a person because of his beliefs.

Read Acts 13:1-4. According to this passage, what had the Church been doing before the Holy Spirit directed them to send out Paul and Barnabas?

_____

_____

_____

Read Acts 10:19-20, 44-48. How did the Holy Spirit reveal to Peter that Gentiles were to be included in His Plan of Redemption?

_____

_____

_____

_____

Read Ephesians 4:1-13. What are the "gifts" listed in this passage? Why were they given to the Church?

_____

_____

_____

When the Spirit of Truth comes, He will lead you into all truth.

(Jn. 16:13a)

❓ Think about it

How has this study affected your understanding of the Church's need for the Holy Spirit?

_____

_____

_____

How will this study affect your thinking about your part in the Church?

_____

_____

_____

How Does He Help Us?
DAY 3

A lost soul cannot be saved without the work of the Holy Spirit. Most of us, as believers, can describe the time and place when someone told us about our need for a Savior. It was the Holy Spirit who brought us to that place and to that witness and prepared our heart to hear. Although the final decision was ours, it was the Holy Spirit who convicted us and led us to repentance and acceptance of God's grace. For lost souls, that is all the Holy Spirit can do.

After we make that decision, the Holy Spirit comes in to abide in our heart and begin the work He will do in us through eternity. He stills our doubts about our salvation and assures us that we truly are born-again children of God. He continues to work, gently and patiently, changing us from the inside, from who we were to who God wants us to be — the likeness of His own Son. To accomplish His purposes, He may work through other believers, but His most effective way is by giving us a hunger for God's Word and speaking to us through it. As we study it, He reveals its great truths to our spirit and shows us how to apply them to our life. Above all, He will lead us to Jesus, for we have much to learn about who we are in Him and all that belongs to us as "joint heirs with Jesus."

God's enemy, Satan, hates God, and He hates all believers and followers of Christ. He knows that the Holy Spirit uses committed Christians to lead unsaved souls out of darkness and into God's Kingdom of Light. Therefore, He brings persecution, oppression and discouragement into our life in an effort to keep us from sharing our faith or to deceive us into turning back into the world and sin. When these times come, we can trust the Holy Spirit to be for us and in us all that Jesus said He would be. If we need comfort, He will be our Comforter. If we need wise advice and direction, He will be our Counselor and our Guide. If we need help, He will be our Helper. When we wander away from the ways of God, as all of us do at times, the Holy Spirit will gently draw us back and teach us how to live to please the Father.

The primary work of the Holy Spirit in each believer is to lead us to a desire to know Jesus. Until we have that desire, He can sustain us, but He can do little more to help us mature spiritually. However, when we finally reach the place where we hunger and thirst for more of Jesus and can be satisfied with nothing less, the Holy Spirit will answer the cry of our heart. He will lead us to empty

KEY SCRIPTURE

If you then, though you are evil, know how to give good gifts to your children, how much more will your Father in heaven give the Holy Spirit to those who ask him!
(Lk. 11:13 NIV)

our life of anything and everything except Jesus. Then He will fill us with the very Spirit of Jesus Himself.

Day by day, He will use the many circumstances and experiences and relationships of our life to produce in us the spiritual fruit that pleases the Father. This is the priceless gift God wants to give every one of His children, because we need the Holy Spirit to help us grow up into Christ.

📖 STUDY THE WORD

Read Luke 11:5-13. How can this scripture assure us the Holy Spirit is for everyone?

_____

_____

_____

Read Acts 2:37-39. What did Peter say we needed to do to receive the gift of the Holy Spirit?

_____

_____

Read John 16:15-16. What are the functions of the Holy Spirit as described in this scripture?

_____

_____

_____

❓ THINK ABOUT IT

How has this study affected your understanding about your own need for the Holy Spirit?

*Holy Spirit,
thou art welcome
in this place.*

_____

_____

_____

What do you believe the Holy Spirit is doing in your life at this time?

_____

_____

_____

How Do We Walk in the Spirit?
DAY 4

Our life here on earth is like a journey. It's as if we're walking along a path, day after day, toward some important destination. This sense of destiny and purpose is unique with man, because God has a plan for every human life — one that we can choose or reject. While we're yet sinners, we're likely to choose to go our own way, seeking to fulfill our own plans and desires, with little concern for anyone else, especially God. However, when our spirit is reborn, this changes — or it should change — dramatically. To the extent that we allow it, the Holy Spirit will work this change in us.

God has a way He wants us to go on our life's journey, but He leaves it entirely up to us to decide whether we will go His way or our own way. After we become born-again children of God, we are new creatures, but we still have much of our "old nature" competing for our allegiance and demanding its way. Going our own way is what the Bible calls "walking in the flesh." The "flesh" offers us what seems to be wonderful freedom and possibilities for pleasure, possessions, popularity, and power. Going God's way offers what seems to be just the opposite. This is Satan's deception, for, despite all we may think or do, we are never in control of our own life. The only choice we have is whether we will be led by him or by the Holy Spirit. Self-rule may be satisfying for a time, but it keeps us on a path that eventually leads to sin and misery. Spirit-rule, on the other hand, is a path that leads to Jesus, and Jesus gives us joy and life and peace.

When we understand this truth, we will realize how important it is for us to choose to walk in the Spirit and to be led by the Spirit. The Holy Spirit wants to be in control of our life, but He can do only what we allow Him to do. If we surrender to His leading, He will teach us how to control the demands of our physical human appetites and our intellect and emotions. The more we surrender to Him, the more of us He can control. The more of us He can control, the more spiritually mature we will become, until we eventually become like Jesus.

Our life journey will lead us through some trials and tribulations that will be like valleys and mountains in our path. We may have to deal with some distressing experiences and difficult circumstances that would hinder us from fulfilling our destiny. The Holy Spirit will teach us how to use the truths of God's

KEY SCRIPTURE

I say then: Walk in the Spirit, and you shall not fulfill the lust of the flesh.
(Gal. 5:16 NKJV)

Word to conquer these trials and tribulations instead of letting them defeat us. We will learn to hear His voice and feel His gentle hand, and we will learn to trust Him and obey Him. If we're to walk in the Spirit, we must surrender daily to His control — body, mind, soul, and spirit. Only He can help us stay on the right path, the one that leads us to God's destination for us.

📖 STUDY THE WORD

Read Romans 8:1-14. How does Paul compare a life controlled by the flesh to one controlled by the Spirit?

_____

_____

_____

Read Galatians 5:16-26. What did Paul say would happen to those who "live according to the flesh"?

_____

_____

_____

Read Ephesians 4:17-24. How does Paul describe the "old self" (old nature, old man) and the "new self" (new nature, new man)?

_____

_____

_____

Spirit of the living God, fall afresh on me. Melt me, mold me, fill me, use me.

❓ THINK ABOUT IT

How has this study affected your understanding about your own "walk in the Spirit"?

_____

_____

_____

_____

Write what you plan to do to become a Spirit-led Christian.

_____

_____

_____

_____

How Do We Use the Spirit's Gifts?
DAY 5

The Church has a tremendous responsibility, and we are the Church. Each of us has a part to play in carrying out the Great Commission. God knew this would require abilities far superior to our own, and He has made a way for us to have everything we need.

The Holy Spirit supplies the Church with general abilities that should operate in every believer's life. He gives us boldness for witnessing, strength to conquer sinful habits, and love and compassion for the lost and needy. He gives revelation knowledge to enable us to understand spiritual truths from God's Word. These general abilities are available to anyone who desires them and will ask for them.

To some, He gives special abilities: inspiration for preaching, teaching, writing, composing music or poetry, or for painting great pictures. In today's world, it may be the special ability to understand and use the latest technology that's needed to spread the Gospel. Whatever it may be, the Holy Spirit wants us to surrender all of our abilities to His control and allow Him to develop them for His purposes.

There are also a variety of spiritual (supernatural) gifts. The Holy Spirit gives these to different people at different times to serve a specific purpose, as He sees fit. Like various parts of the physical body, each gift has a necessary function. The Spirit's gifts are not a reward for righteousness or payment for service and are certainly not for proving the spiritual maturity of the person operating them. They're gifts — enabling, empowering gifts — always to be used for the common good of the Church and always to bring glory and honor to Jesus — not man. Some gifts are for ministering healing and deliverance to fellow believers. Some come as supernatural words of wisdom, knowledge and faith to encourage and strengthen the Church. Often, it will be a gift of discernment to help us know what is of God and what is not of God.

The New Testament gives many examples of spiritual gifts being used. For example, although He was the Son of God, Jesus emptied Himself of His divine powers when He came to earth. He lived as a man, but as a Spirit-filled, Spirit-led man. He showed His disciples (and us) how these powerful gifts are supposed to operate in the life of any Spirit-filled, Spirit-led believer. He

KEY SCRIPTURE
But the natural, nonspiritual man does not accept or welcome or admit into his heart the gifts and teachings and revelations of the Spirit of God, for they are folly (meaningless nonsense) to him; and he is incapable of knowing them…because they are spiritually discerned….
(1 Cor. 2:15 AMP)

preached with great power, healed the sick, cast out demons, raised the dead, and performed miracles. After the Day of Pentecost, the same spiritual gifts operated in the lives of His Spirit-filled, Spirit-led followers, just as Jesus had said they would. The New Testament is a record of their ministries.

Every member of the Body of Christ has at least one spiritual gift, and, if we ask Him, the Holy Spirit will show us what it is and how we're to use it. However, there are conditions for using His gifts, and the Holy Spirit will judge our readiness by the condition of our heart and the intensity of our desire to glorify Jesus and obey His voice.

📖 STUDY THE WORD

Read 1 Corinthians 2:6-16. How does Paul compare the "spiritual man" with the "nonspiritual man"?

_____

_____

_____

Read Romans 12:3-16. What should be our attitude about the various spiritual "gifts" in the Body of Christ?

_____

_____

_____

Read 1 Corinthians 12:1-27. With what does Paul compare the spiritual "gifts" and the way they should be used in the Body of Christ?

_____

_____

For the gifts and the calling of God are irrevocable.

(Rom.11:29 NKJV)

❓ THINK ABOUT IT

How has this study affected your understanding about spiritual gifts?

_____

_____

What do you believe is your spiritual gift? How you will use it to edify the Church?

_____

_____

UNIT 5 What Is Not True Faith?

Why Is Faith So Important?
DAY 1

It takes faith to please God. What the Word teaches about God and about Jesus demands a response from each of us. Will we accept what it says as final authority? Will we submit our life to its truths? Absolutely everything in our life is affected, directly or indirectly, by the way we answer that question. The spiritual world is very real — more real than anything we can experience with our senses; but it is not manifested to our senses. We must accept everything about it strictly by faith. By faith we choose to believe in an invisible God and to love Him with all our heart, mind, soul and strength. By faith we choose to accept Jesus as our Redeemer. If we can't please God without faith, then He must, in all fairness, make it possible for us to get it. If He gives us the means whereby we can develop faith, then the responsibility rests with us to learn how to get it and use it to please Him. Our quest for spiritual maturity, then, continues with a search to learn all we possibly can about faith.

It takes faith to be saved. Every sin of every man, woman and child in the entire world was washed in the blood of Jesus Christ. God's desire is for all to be saved from the terrible penalty of those sins and to become part of His eternal family. Apart from His Word, however, we have no way of proving the truth of this message. God, in His wisdom, has granted us the freedom to make a choice. When we hear this Good News (the Gospel message), we must either believe it by faith or refuse to believe it and continue to live in the kingdom of darkness. Paul speaks of the need for faith for salvation in many of his letters.

It takes faith to live victoriously. Despite constantly improving technology, life is becoming more stressful for each generation. We face potential danger all around us every day. Crime, terrorism, incurable diseases, social and economic problems — all seem to defy any governmental solutions. No one is immune from tragic events that can change our life in a moment. It's what we believe in our heart that determines whether such difficulties leave us defeated or victorious. Love, joy, peace, and freedom from every form of bondage — these belong to us, and we have every right to enjoy them while we live out our life on this planet. Although Jesus defeated Satan, it is our responsibility to enforce this defeat in our own life and in the Body of Christ. The Holy Spirit gives us everything we need to keep him from robbing us of our inheritance. Accepting

KEY SCRIPTURE

Without faith it is impossible to please Him; for he who comes to God must believe that He is, and that He is a rewarder of those who diligently seek him.
(Heb. 11:6 NKJV)

The LORD taketh pleasure in them that fear him, in those that hope in his mercy.
(Ps. 147:11 KJV)

I am not ashamed of the gospel of Christ: for it is the power of God unto salvation to every one that believeth, to the Jew first, and also to the Greek, for therein is the righteousness of God revealed from faith to faith: as it is written, The just shall live by faith.
(Rom. 1:16-17 KJV)

Whatever is born of God overcomes the world. And this is the victory that has overcomes the world — our faith. Who is he who overcome the world, but he who believes that Jesus is the Son of God?
(1 Jn. 5:4-5 NKJV)

this responsibility and living as a conqueror over Satan requires strong faith on our part — a faith built upon a solid, never-changing foundation.

📖 STUDY THE WORD

Read Luke 7:1-10. What was Jesus' response to the faith of the centurion?

_____

_____

_____

_____

Read 1 Peter 1:3-9. How did Peter describe the value of faith?

_____

_____

_____

_____

Read Romans 3:21-31. Why did Paul say there was no longer any difference between those who kept the law and those who did not?

_____

_____

_____

_____

_____

❓ THINK ABOUT IT

How has this study helped you understand the importance of faith?

_____

_____

_____

_____

_____

How does this study change your priorities?

_____

_____

_____

_____

This is the victory that overcomes the world — our faith.
(I Jn. 5:4)

Faith Is Not Mental Assent or Acceptance of Physical Evidence
DAY 2

What does the word "faith" mean? If we ask that question in any group of people, even a group of Christians, we're likely to get a different answer from each person. The very mention of the term may bring a variety of reactions — guilt, pride, evasion, envy, and even anger. That's because there are widespread misconceptions about what faith is and what it means to us personally. Unfortunately, some of these ideas have been around so long and have been taught so thoroughly that they are deeply rooted in minds and hearts.

If we're to grow into the likeness of Christ, we need to clear up this confusion. Furthermore, because our faith tends to weaken under pressure, it helps to refresh our commitment to the basic truths of God's Word, regardless of where we are in our maturing process. In order to live victoriously on this earth, we must find out what faith is, how to develop it, and how to apply it. Before we can study what faith IS, we need to look at some of these misleading thought patterns.

Faith is not mental assent. Many people will tell us they believe the Bible is true, but agreeing with factual information is not faith. Accepting the existence of God is an important first step, but it is not enough. Acknowledging that Jesus Christ came to earth and that He died on a cross is an important step toward salvation, but it will not be enough until we receive Him as our own personal Savior and Lord. Even demonic spirits recognized Jesus as the Son of God.

Faith is not acceptance of physical evidence. Thomas, one of Jesus' disciples, had heard Him preach and teach and had watched Him perform miracles for three years. Yet, Thomas refused to believe that Jesus was alive unless he could prove it himself by touching the wounds in Jesus' hands and side. Thomas believed with natural human faith, based on physical evidence that could be explained or experienced by the senses. Everyone — even the non-Christian — has this kind of faith concerning laws of nature and science. For example, we have faith that, when we plug an appliance cord into an outlet, we're going to get electrical power to operate the appliance. We may not understand all the principles of electricity, but we believe that provable scientific laws are working. Any kind of law should work every time it's applied. This kind of faith is based on knowledge and experience.

KEY SCRIPTURE
You believe that God is one; and you do well. Even the demons believe — and shudder.
(Jam. 2:19 RSV)

Jesus saith unto him, Thomas, because thou hast seen me, thou hast believed: blessed are they that have not seen, and yet have believed.
(Jn. 20:29 KJV)

Most of us sincerely want to be people of faith, but how can we know whether our belief is truly faith and not merely mental agreement? We will likely not know the answer to that question until what we believe is put to the test. Eventually, we will face some situation that requires a response on our part. Mental agreement will give way to reasoning or will wait for further confirmation. Faith will lean heavily upon what God says in His Word.

UNDERSTANDING THE TERMS
mental assent or agreement: accepting something on the basis of observable evidence or past experience.

physical evidence: proof that can be experienced with the senses.

📖 STUDY THE WORD

Read John 20:19-29. What did Jesus say to Thomas when He first appeared to Thomas after the resurrection? How did Thomas respond?

_____

_____

_____

_____

_____

Read Luke 17:11-19. This is the story of the healing of the ten lepers. Compare the faith of the one who returned and the nine who did not.

_____

_____

_____

_____

❓ THINK ABOUT IT

What confusion do you have about the meaning of faith?

_____

_____

_____

_____

_____

There is no faith in believing what you can see or prove.

Before further study about faith, write what you think it means.

_____

_____

_____

_____

_____

Faith Is Not Works or Special Abilities
DAY 3

Faith is not a talent or special ability, although many people tend to think of it that way — as if it is a special, God-given endowment. For example, some people can sing well; some cannot. Some people can be leaders; some can't be leaders but do other things well. While there are times when the Holy Spirit will grant a special gift of faith to meet a specific need, we should not confuse it with the kind of faith we need for daily living. We all hear comments like these: "I really admire his faith…." or "If I had as much faith as you do…." or "Some have faith and some don't."

Thomas' personality and abilities had nothing to do with his faith. To believe or not believe was his own choice. When Jesus healed someone, he often said, "Your faith has made you whole." He did not say or imply, "Because God has given you special faith, I will heal you." If faith is not available to everyone equally, then God would not expect us to manifest it equally.

Faith is not works. A scripture in the book of James teaches that "Faith without works is dead." Many people have used this scripture to equate faith with "church work" or doing good deeds. Service can, of course, be an evidence of faith, as in the case of tithing and giving. However, this is not to be a substitute for faith in God and His Word. This is what Jesus found wrong in the Pharisees of His day. Because they were expecting their "good works" to prove them righteous before God, they saw no reason to believe in Jesus, Who often appeared to be breaking the law.

There is a "work of the Lord" for all Christians to do. The disciples asked Jesus, "What must we do, to be doing the works of God?" Jesus replied, "This is the work of God, that you believe in him whom he has sent" (Jn. 6:28-29 RSV). The "work of the Lord," then, is BELIEVING in the Anointed One sent from God.

While many good people do a great deal of much-needed "church work," that does not necessarily indicate they have great faith. The Apostle Paul encouraged believers in the Church to "abound in the work of the Lord." He recognized the need for laborers who would spend their lives either spreading the gospel or supporting those who did. Persons of strong faith are often the ones who do this kind of labor, and it will surely reap a heavenly reward; but the work itself is not faith.

➡◯ KEY SCRIPTURE

Therefore, my beloved brethren, be steadfast, immovable, always abounding in the work of the Lord, knowing that your labor is not in vain in the Lord.
(1 Cor. 15:58 NKJV)

This is the work of God, that ye believe on him whom he hath sent.
(Jn. 6:29b KJV)

As children of God, we no longer live under the Law of Moses. We now live under the law of grace. Nothing we can possibly do will earn for us any more of God's love and favor than He already has toward us. Therefore, we serve Him, not to convince Him (and others) of our faith, but because we love Him and want to show His love to the world. Anything worthwhile that we do is what He does THROUGH us, not what we do FOR Him. It is far better for us to bear good fruit, which will inevitably lead to doing good works, than to do good works expecting the works to produce more faith.

📖 STUDY THE WORD

Read Romans 9:30-33. Why did Paul say that salvation by faith in Jesus was a "stumbling stone" to Israel?

_____

_____

_____

_____

UNDERSTANDING THE TERMS

grace: undeserved forgiveness, love and favor.

works: activities taken to help the Church or those who spread the Gospel.

Read Ephesians 2:8-10. What does Paul say about faith and works in this scripture?

_____

_____

_____

_____

_____

_____

❓ THINK ABOUT IT

What "works" have you sometimes confused with true faith?

_____

_____

_____

_____

Faith may produce good works, but good works do not produce faith.

How does this study change your thinking about your own "works"?

_____

_____

Faith Is Not Hope
DAY 4

Hope is not in any way inferior to faith, but we can build a stronger faith when we understand that they are different. Most of us tend to use the two terms interchangeably until we understand what true faith actually is. Hope, as most of us use it, is not faith, and only true faith can claim and receive the blessings of God for victorious living. To simplify the difference, we could say that hope looks for answers "someday." Faith is now — something already done and assured. Hope says, "Maybe God will." Faith says, "He has." Hope tends to leave room for God to refuse and gives us a rationalization, an "out," in case He doesn't "come through" for us. Faith needs no excuse; it takes God at His Word. God Himself spoke of what He was going to do as if He had already done it. Many years before Abraham had even one son, God told him, "I HAVE made thee a great nation." (Gen. 17:1-5) He told Joshua before the battle had even begun, "I HAVE delivered into thy hand Jericho." (Josh. 6:2) In the story of David and Goliath, we can see that hope could have left David fearful of what MIGHT happen. However, because God had delivered him from other enemies, David KNEW (not hoped) there would be victory again. (1 Sam. 17:34-37)

Hope does have a very important function, and we should not take it lightly. It is absolutely necessary to our well-being. One of the most disturbing problems in any nation in any age is hopelessness. If we could get even a fleeting glimpse of hell and those who've gone there, we would surely see that hopelessness is one of the most grievous of the torments they suffer. We have hope in the soon return of our Lord Jesus Christ, for the rapture of the Church, and for the resurrection of the righteous. We hope for the home in heaven where we will see loved ones again. The hope we have in Jesus should give rise to unending praise.

While God wants us to hope for these things, we know that they will happen whether we have faith or not. Jesus IS coming. The resurrection WILL take place. Our faith or lack of it will not have any effect upon it. This is hope. It is NOT faith, and it will not change anything. That takes faith. Sometimes, in a time of distress, we'll say, "All I can do now is hope and pray." This kind of thinking can produce defeat and disappointment and can do little to change the situation. The situation requires, instead, a strong faith that goes beyond hope for the future and believes the truth of God's Word for today's need.

🔑 KEY SCRIPTURE

For everything that was written in the past was written to teach us, so that through endurance and the encouragement of the Scriptures we might have hope. (Rom. 15:4 NIV)

Faith believes that what God has promised to do, He WILL do, REGARDLESS OF CIRCUMSTANCES. It will become fact, or has already become fact, BECAUSE of faith and BEFORE it can be proved in any way. It is possible to build such a faith, and this is a big part of our quest for spiritual maturity.

📖 **STUDY THE WORD**

Read 1 Thessalonians 1:1-10. When Paul prayed for the people in this church, what did he remember about them that gave him cause for gratitude?

_____

_____

_____

_____

UNDERSTANDING THE TERMS
hope: confident expectation, which has to do with the unseen and the future.

Study 1 Samuel 17. What did David say, as he faced the giant, that indicates he was acting in faith — not hope?

_____

_____

_____

Study Psalm 23. Give special attention to the tense of the verbs. What can they tell you about the Psalmist's faith?

_____

_____

_____

_____

? **THINK ABOUT IT**

How has this study changed your understanding of hope?

_____

_____

_____

Those who hope in the LORD will renew their strength.
(Isa. 40:31 NIV)

How does this study change the way you pray?

_____

_____

_____

Faith Is Not a Feeling or a Magic Wand
DAY 5

Faith is not an emotion. Just as our body can experience a variety of symptoms, our soul can produce a variety of emotions. Emotions and feelings are manifestations of our reactions to whatever is going on around us. They're part of our human nature, and have nothing to do with faith. Man is spirit, and faith rises from our spirit — the part of us that is like God — not from our human nature. We can feel "up" one moment and "down" the next moment. While it is possible to have impressions about what is taking place in the spirit, we cannot feel faith. Faith believes on the basis of the Word alone, despite feelings or symptoms. For example, sometimes we may feel that God is very close; sometimes we may feel as if He's far away. And yet, He SAID, "I will never leave thee nor forsake thee." (Heb. 13:5-6) We can believe, then, that He IS with us, regardless of how we feel at the moment. A mature believer of strong faith may be experiencing some heart-wrenching tragedy and yet be at peace in his spirit. He can do that because he has determined to cast the burden of grief and pain so completely upon God that his emotions will not be his master in the situation. Feelings can lead to doubt and fear. Therefore, faith never allows emotions to be a consideration in spiritual matters or in receiving blessings from God.

Faith is not a magic wand. It's easy to slip into thinking of God as we would think of some kind of benefactor or genie, waiting to hear our latest wish or demand. Faith is not saying just the right words in just the right way in an effort to get God to do something for us that He's loathe to do. Such a magic-wand mentality places our faith in OUR words and OUR methods instead of in what God has said in His Word and has already done in the spiritual realm.

Faith is powerful, but we must not get to the place of "using" God. Nor should we depend upon our own or any other person's skill or position to receive from Him. Our human nature is so frail and our tendency toward pride and self-seeking is so strong that it could bring about disastrous results. The Apostle Paul recognized this and admitted that it was a danger in his own life and ministry and warned against it in the Church. The Holy Spirit wants to develop in each of us a relationship with God that keeps us constantly aware of our total dependence upon Him and Him alone for any blessings we seek. Answers to prayers do not always come quickly and according to our own expectations.

KEY SCRIPTURE

Peter said to him, "Your money perish with you, because you thought that the gift of God could be purchased with money! You have neither part nor portion in this matter, for your heart is not right in the sight of God.
(Acts 8:20-21 NKJV)

Even mature Christians experience times when it seems as if their prayers are not reaching heaven at all. At such times, we must rely on the wisdom of our Heavenly Father. Only He knows what is best for us and how much we can successfully handle at our level of maturity.

📖 STUDY THE WORD

Read Mark 10:46-52. It was not his excitement that brought healing for blind Bartemeus. What did he do that indicated he had faith for it?

_____

_____

_____

_____

UNDERSTANDING THE TERMS
emotions: specific feelings with both mental and physical manifestations.

magic wand: anything thought to have power to perform supernatural miracles.

Study Acts 8:1-25. Simon the Sorcerer offered to pay the apostles. What did they have that he wanted? What was Peter's reply?

_____

_____

_____

_____

Study Acts 19:11-20. What happened to those who tried to perform miracles apart from faith in God?

_____

_____

_____

❓ THINK ABOUT IT

How has this study changed the way you think about feelings?

_____

_____

_____

_____

Faith grows out of the spirit — not the soul — of man.

How does this study change the way you pray?

_____

_____

_____

_____

UNIT 6 What Is True Faith?

Faith Is a Decision to Believe God
DAY 1

Our quest brings us to a study of what God-pleasing, victorious faith actually is. When we understand these principles of biblical faith, we will experience a great deal more power in our prayer life, and it will open the door for greater blessings from God and service for God. The writer of Hebrews gives us an excellent definition of faith. If we read it from several translations, we learn that faith is substance, evidence, confidence, assurance, conviction, and certainty.

- Now faith is the SUBSTANCE of things hoped for, the EVIDENCE of things not seen. (KJV)
- Faith is the ASSURANCE of things hoped for, the CONVICTION of things not seen. (RSV)
- What is faith? It is the CONFIDENT ASSURANCE that something we want is going to happen. It is the CERTAINTY that what we hope for is waiting for us, even though we cannot see it up ahead. (TLB)

Throughout His ministry, Jesus taught that He was the Anointed One, promised by the prophets, sent from God to destroy the works of the devil. He brought reconciliation, peace with God, release from the bondage of sin, and eternal life for all who would believe. When He returned to the Father, He left the same message for His disciples to take to the world. Now, as then, some hear the message, choose to believe it, and accept all that Jesus did for them by His death on the cross. Some hear and, for one reason or another, CHOOSE to reject the truth of it and go their own way. Each person who chooses to believe becomes a new creation and enters into a new relationship with God. Now he can testify to others about the truth of the Gospel message and the grace of God. Yet, while there may be obvious changes in his life, he cannot offer his listeners any tangible proof of what has happened to him as a result of his faith. Each one who hears his testimony must decide whether to believe and accept it or to doubt and reject it.

This same faith is required to receive any of God's promises. Deep within the spirit, there must be a no-turning-back decision to agree with the Word of God, regardless of circumstances. Faith needs no evidence. When all the evidence says "no" but God says "yes," faith will agree and trust in the integrity of God. The person who chooses faith understands that the real fact is not necessarily

KEY SCRIPTURE
He did not weaken in faith, when he considered the [utter] impotence of his own body, which was as good as dead because he was about a hundred years old, or [when he considered] the barrenness of Sarah's (deadened) womb. No unbelief or distrust made him waver [doubtingly question] concerning the promise of God, but he grew strong and was EMPOWERED BY FAITH as he gave praise and glory to God, fully satisfied and assured that God was able and mighty to keep His word and to do what He had promised.
(Rom. 4:19-21 AMP)

what his senses tell him; faith counts things done BEFORE God has acted. Abraham is called the "Father of Faith" for this very reason, and he is an excellent example of this kind of faith. The terms "considered" and "fully satisfied" and "assured" describe characteristics of strong faith. Abraham was able to give praise to God because of his trust in the wisdom, power, and faithfulness of God. He KNEW God would keep His promise.

📖 STUDY THE WORD

Read Deuteronomy 1:19-46. This is an example of a decision that affected the entire nation of Israel. What was that decision?

_____

_____

_____

_____

Read Deuteronomy 30:1-20. What choice did Moses offer God's people? Who would be affected by their choice?

_____

_____

_____

_____

Read Romans 4:13-21. Why do the promises of God have to come by faith and not by keeping the Law?

_____

_____

_____

❓ THINK ABOUT IT

Faith is confident trust in someone or something. How does this definition change your thinking about your own faith in God?

_____

_____

_____

_____

_____

_____

UNDERSTANDING THE TERMS

the will: the power of deliberate choice.

faith: loyalty to a person; confidence in the word of another; unwavering trust and confidence.

trust: firm confidence in the honesty, integrity, reliability and justice of another person.

Choose you this day whom you will serve.
(Josh. 24:15)

Faith Is a Very Real Force
DAY 2

Faith is a powerful spiritual law — a very real force. God used this spiritual law and applied His own faith when He spoke the commands that created the universe. This should be convincing evidence of the tremendous power of faith. God KNEW what His Words could and would do when He spoke the world into being from nothingness. He had absolute confidence in the power of His own words.

When Jesus was on earth, He often said to someone, "Your faith has made you whole." By this, He was implying that the person had SOMETHING that made the healing possible. In fact, Jesus always spoke of faith as if it were a substance or force that could DO things. Like any force, then, it can be strong or weak, and it can be developed or left dormant and inactive. Like any law, it can be expected to work every time it's applied. Jesus taught this very clearly and demonstrated it throughout His ministry. He healed crippled bodies and blind eyes by speaking life and wholeness into them. He commanded storms to cease and multiplied food to feed thousands. He wanted His listeners to learn that this kind of faith is capable of making real changes when it's applied with sufficient strength.

The power of faith is just as important and just as available to believers today as it was in Jesus' day. Since God's nature abides in our spirit, faith is now part of our nature. However, our faith at any given moment may be weak or strong. We can develop it or leave it dormant and inactive. Jesus wants all of His followers to understand the power of this force and learn to apply it for His purposes. He said we could speak to a mountain and it would move, or we could speak to a tree and it would be uprooted. It takes a considerable amount of force to move a mountain into the sea or to uproot a tree, but Jesus said that our faith, properly applied, could make it happen. Faith, then, can undoubtedly be a very real force in our hands.

Before He went back to heaven, Jesus told His disciples (and us) that supernatural signs would follow believers. They would heal the sick and cast out demons in His name. In fact, He said we would be doing even greater things than He had done. Healing the sick and casting out demons, like moving mountains and trees, are miracles that require supernatural power. Yet, Jesus always phrased His promises emphatically. He said they WOULD (not might) take place for those who would believe.

KEY SCRIPTURE

Jesus answering saith unto them, Have faith in God. For verily I say unto you, That whosoever shall say unto this mountain, Be thou removed and be thou cast into the sea; and shall not doubt in his heart, but shall believe that those things which he saith shall come to pass; he shall have whatsoever he saith. (Mk. 11:22-23 KJV)

The apostles said unto the Lord, Increase our faith. And the Lord said, If ye had faith as a grain of mustard seed, ye might say unto this sycamine tree, Be thou plucked up by the root, and be thou planted in the sea; and it should obey you (Lk. 17:5-6 KJV)

These signs shall follow them that believe: In my name shall they cast out devils; they shall speak with new tongues; They shall take up serpents; and if they drink any deadly thing, it shall not hurt them; they shall lay hands on the sick, and they shall recover. (Mk. 16:17-18 KJV)

What is it that we are to believe? We must believe that every promise in the Word is as valid today as it was when it was first breathed by God through His anointed writers. This kind of bold faith should be the desire of every Christian, regardless of age, position, or past experiences. The Church needs this kind of power in these last days, if we're to fulfill God's plans for saving the lost.

📖 STUDY THE WORD

Read Joshua 6:1-20. Whose faith produced the tremendous power that destroyed the walls of Jericho?

_____

_____

_____

_____

UNDERSTANDING THE TERMS

force: the exertion of power in causing a thing to act, move, or comply against a resistance.

evidence: indication of proof.

confidence: reliance; trust.

assurance: guarantee; pledge.

substance: matter; material.

Read 1 Kings 18:20-46. This is the story of a mighty miracle that took place on Mt. Carmel. What was Elijah's part in it?

_____

_____

_____

_____

Read Acts 3:1-16. This is an account of a miraculous healing. What did Peter say was the reason for the miracle?

_____

_____

_____

_____

❓ THINK ABOUT IT

How does this study affect your thinking about the power of faith?

God specializes in things thought impossible.

_____

_____

_____

_____

_____

_____

Faith Is Life
DAY 3

Sin came into the world through Adam, and with sin came death, sickness, disease, and everything else that's part of dying. Jesus came to bring life to this sinful world, but we cannot purchase it or earn it in any way. This life is a gift to anyone and everyone who will choose to believe it is theirs. Therefore, we can accurately say that "Faith IS life."

This makes it quite clear that the choice is left to each individual who hears the message of salvation through Jesus. The consequences of the choice are also dramatically clear — believe and live; refuse to believe and perish. On the basis of our scriptures from the Gospel of John, we can understand that if we choose to believe in what Jesus has done, eternal life (and everything it involves) has already begun for us. It does not wait to begin when our existence on earth is over.

Everyone lives by faith in something or someone. It may be faith in our own abilities, in our financial security, in the government, or whatever determines our lifestyle. We have an example of this in the Apostle Paul. He had always lived by faith, but his faith was in the Law. The Law had been his life. After Jesus became real to him on the road to Damascus, everything in Paul's life changed. Spiritually, he "died" that day, and Paul was born — a new man with a new spirit and a new zeal. From that day, he began to live by a new faith — a faith based on a Person. He said, "the life I now live in the body, I live by faith in the Son of God." (Gal. 2:20 NIV)

A child growing up in a good family with positive influences should eventually come to a place where he can trust his parents' word to be true, regardless of any circumstances that may make it seem otherwise. Trust will not be an on-again-off-again matter. He will not believe their word some days but doubt their truthfulness on other days. The more mature he becomes, the more this trust will develop into a way of life and a basis for his peace and security. It should be the same with God's children, growing up in His Kingdom. The more we grow spiritually, the more stable we should be in our trust in the integrity of our Father and His Word. Our faith will be life to us — in every sense of that word. Jesus has already set us free from everything in this life that was the result of "the law of sin and death." We can walk in as much of this blessing and freedom as we choose to believe we have. What we choose to believe, or choose not to

KEY SCRIPTURE

God so loved the world, that he gave his only begotten Son, that whosoever believeth in him should not perish, but have everlasting life.
(Jn. 3:16 KJV)

This is the will of him that sent me, that every one which seeth the Son, and believeth on him, may have everlasting life: and I will raise him up at the last day.
(Jn. 6:40 KJV)

There is therefore now no condemnation to them which are in Christ Jesus, who walk not after the flesh, but after the Spirit. For the law of the Spirit of life in Christ Jesus hath made me free from the law of sin and death.
(Rom. 8:1-2 KJV)

Behold, he whose soul is not upright in him shall fail, but the righteous shall live by his faith.
(Hab. 2:4 RSV)

believe, about Jesus and what He did for us on the cross, will affect every area of our life. That includes our physical, mental, emotional, spiritual, financial and social well being. Our faith in Him will become not only life itself, but also a way of living day by day.

📖 **STUDY THE WORD**

Read John 6:52-63. How do we receive all the benefits of Jesus' life?

_____

_____

_____

_____

Read John 17:3. Write the definition of eternal life according to Jesus.

_____

_____

_____

_____

Read Acts 3:15-16. According to this scripture, who is the author of life?

_____

_____

_____

_____

_____

_____

UNDERSTANDING THE TERMS

life: that which God has in Himself, and which the Son manifested to the world. We become partakers of it through faith in Jesus.

way of life: the pattern of thought that governs our actions and reactions to daily events.

? **THINK ABOUT IT**

How does this study change the way you think about faith and your own life?

_____

_____

_____

_____

_____

_____

_____

_____

_____

I am the Way, and the Truth and the Life.
(Jn. 14:6 AMP)

Faith Is a Gift from God
DAY 4

One of the most vital facts that each of us must understand about faith is that it does not arise from our mind. It grows up out of our spirit, the part of us the Bible often calls our "heart" or our "inner man." We see this in several passages of scripture.

- In Mark 11:23, Jesus said, "…and shall not doubt in his heart…."
- In Romans 10:10, Paul said, "For with the heart man believeth unto righteousness."
- In Proverbs 3:5-8, we read, "Trust in the Lord with all thine heart and lean not unto thine own understanding…."

The word "heart," as used in these scriptures, means the innermost part of our being, the part around which all the rest revolves. We've learned that man is spirit, created in the image of his Creator God, Who is spirit. From the moment of our conception, each of us enters life, and we will continue to exist forever, even after our time on earth is over. Unlike other creatures on this planet, we have the privilege of knowing our Creator and communicating with Him. However, we must know Him and relate to Him in our spirit, for He does not manifest Himself to our senses. It's up to us, then, either to choose to believe in this God we cannot see, or to choose to believe only what we can understand with our mind and experience through our senses.

To believe with the heart is often to believe APART from what our physical body or our senses tell us. Often it must go AGAINST logic or common sense. Our natural human mind simply cannot understand spiritual concepts such as "born again," "being one with the Father and the Son," or "I am with you always." Yet, without being able to see, hear, feel, or understand, we can have a "knowing" in our spirit. When we choose to act on this knowing, we're acting on faith.

How can we get to this place where our spirit can believe, even when our mind cannot understand? As we've seen, faith is not some kind of special ability that God deals out to some in great measure and to others in small doses. We're not creatures of mere instinct, as other created lifeforms are. God gives every believer the ability to believe as part of our free will. Faith, then, is a gift from God's Spirit to our spirit. Everyone who accepts Jesus as Savior can say, "Even the faith with which I believe for salvation is a gift from God."

🔑 **KEY SCRIPTURE**

The natural man receiveth not the things of the Spirit of God: for they are foolishness unto him: neither can he know them, because they are spiritually discerned.
(1 Cor. 2:14 KJV)

The fruit of the Spirit is love, joy, peace, longsuffering, gentleness, goodness, FAITH…If we live in the Spirit, let us also walk in the Spirit.
(from Gal. 5:22-25 KJV)

By grace are ye saved through faith; and that not of yourselves: it is the gift of God.
(Eph. 2:8 KJV)

…according as God hath dealt to every man the measure of faith.
(Rom. 12:13 KJV)

Read Ephesians 2:1-9. Why did Paul say that we can't even boast about our salvation?

_____

_____

_____

_____

_____

_____

Read Proverbs 3:5-8. How does this scripture confirm the truth that faith comes from the spirit?

_____

_____

_____

_____

_____

_____

Read Romans 12:1-8. According to this scripture, how was the "measure of faith" supposed to be used by believers in the Church?

_____

_____

_____

_____

_____

_____

❓ **THINK ABOUT IT**

How does this study change the way you think about your own "measure of faith"?

Faith is a gift from God's heart to our heart.

_____

_____

_____

_____

_____

_____

Faith Is Trusting the Word of God
DAY 5

When we feed our physical body the right kind of food, we say we're "healthy." When we provide knowledge, study and training for our mind, we say we're "educated." When we establish spiritual truths in our spirit, we can say we're "developing faith." Faith comes by hearing the Word of God and allowing the Holy Spirit to reveal its truths to our spirit. The scriptures are quite clear about this. The spirit of man feeds on divine truths from the Word of God. When we take food into our body, we may not know exactly what happens, but it gives life to our physical body. Just so, when we take the Word of God into our spirit, we don't know how it's processed, but it gives life to our spirit.

As we feed our spirit with powerful truths from the Word of God, the force of faith can quicken our spirit and bring life and health to our entire being — body, soul and spirit. The New Testament gives many examples of faith that produced miracles. In each case, the miracle or miracles came as a result of someone hearing the truth, believing it, and acting upon what they believed to be true. Here are two such examples.

> • In Acts 8:5-8, we read the story of Philip in Samaria. The great miracles recorded in these verses came about because Philip preached a message of salvation in Jesus Christ, which includes physical healing. The listeners who chose to believe received miracles of healing and deliverance.

> • In Mk. 5:24-34, we read the story of Jesus healing the woman with an issue of blood. "And he said unto her, Daughter, thy faith hath made thee whole; go in peace, and be whole of thy plague." (v. 34) Jesus said it was HER faith that overcame the physical condition. Undoubtedly, she had heard Jesus preach, and she believed that healing belonged to her. Her believing activated this truth and quickened her body. She could go KNOWING it was done.

Jesus gave us the key to this kind of faith when He said, "you will know the truth, and the truth will set you free." (Jn. 8:32 TLB) Truth is there for us in Jesus and all that He has done for us, but it cannot set us free until we KNOW that truth and CHOOSE TO BELIEVE IT in our heart. The Holy Spirit reveals a truth to us from the Word, perhaps a promise that belongs to us under the

KEY SCRIPTURE

It is the Spirit who gives life; the flesh profits nothing. The words that I speak to you are spirit, and they are life.
(Jn. 6:63 NKJV)

So then faith cometh by hearing, and hearing by the word of God.
(Rom. 10:17 KJV)

My son, attend to my words; incline thine ear unto my sayings. Let them not depart from thine eyes; keep them in the midst of thine heart. For they are life unto those that find them, and health to all their flesh. Keep thy heart with all diligence; for out of it are the issues of life.
(Prov. 4:20-23 KJV)

Blood Covenant. As we meditate on that truth, the Holy Spirit shows us how it applies to some seemingly impossible "mountain" that needs to be moved in our circumstances. Eventually, mental agreement and hope will give way to a deeply rooted assurance. This is faith that can change the circumstances and bring the victory.

📖 STUDY THE WORD

Read Acts 14:7-10. In this story of the healing of a crippled man, what was the man's part in his healing?

_____
_____
_____
_____

Read Romans 10:8-21. What does this scripture tell us is the source of faith?

_____
_____
_____
_____
_____

Read Acts 4:1-4. Peter preached a sermon to the crowd. What was their response? What was the result of their response?

_____
_____
_____
_____
_____

? THINK ABOUT IT

How does this study change the way you think about your Bible?

_____
_____
_____
_____
_____

We are only as free as the truth we know.

UNIT 7 How Do We Use Faith?

Remember Who Lives in Us
DAY 1

The Church needs believers of strong faith today, perhaps more than any other time in history. Satanic forces, knowing their time is limited, are filling the world with evil as never before, and Christians are not immune to their deceptions. God's purpose for the Church is to show His love to the world by telling them what Jesus has done for them. Yet, most of us find that our faith is barely strong enough to fight our own personal battles. We're attacked in our bodies, in our families, in our businesses, and everywhere else Satan can find an opportunity. One of the reasons for this is that we forget who we are and try to fight our battles as if we are still who we used to be.

Throughout the Word of God, we find countless references to "the world." We must understand that only in a few cases does this term refer to the planet Earth. Rather, in Scripture "the world" may represent all of humanity that is not yet part of God's Kingdom. It includes the entire system of life that is still under satanic control. In spiritual realms, this world and the Kingdom of God are hopelessly at enmity with one another. The people in each of those kingdoms are experiencing the trauma of unending warfare.

When a lost soul hears the Gospel message, believes it and accepts salvation through faith in Jesus Christ, he moves out of Satan's kingdom of darkness and into God's Kingdom of Light. However, like a newborn child, he has much to learn about life as a citizen of this new realm. While he's learning, he will likely go through many difficult attacks that will "try" his faith. Every one of us, as believers, could agree with this and testify about our own struggles.

Until Jesus returns to take the Church out of the world, we can expect these attacks to continue and even intensify. That should help us understand that our quest for spiritual maturity is essential, for we must learn how to live more victoriously. We must remember that we are not fighting our battles with our own skills and our own strength. We live IN Christ, and He lives IN us. We fight with the weapons He supplies, and we need to learn how to use them skillfully. On the night before He died, Jesus told his disciples, "Abide in me like branches abide on a vine." Then He prayed a remarkable prayer that includes all believers in all generations. He asked the Father to make us one with Him as He is one

---

KEY SCRIPTURE

Little children, you are of God [you belong to Him] and have [already] defeated and overcome them [the agents of antichrist], because He Who lives in you is greater (mightier) than he who is in the world.
(1 Jn. 4:4 AMP)

For in Him the whole fullness of Deity (the Godhead) continues to dwell in bodily form [giving complete expression of the divine nature]. And you are in Him, made full and having come to fullness of life [in Christ you too are filled with the Godhead — Father, Son and Holy Spirit — and reach full spiritual stature]. And He is the Head of all rule and authority [of every angelic principality and power].
(Col. 2:9-10 AMP)

If you belonged to the world, the world would treat you with affection and would love you as its own. But because you are not of the world [are no longer one with it,] but I have chosen (selected) you out of the world, the world hates (detests) you.
(John 15:19 AMP)

with the Father. When the disciples grasped the awesome truth of who they were in Jesus Christ, they became apostles, fearlessly meeting all of Satan's attacks against the Church. As unthinkable as it may seem to us, the Father is in Jesus, Jesus is in us, and that means we are one with the Godhead. We are fully supported by all the authority of the Kingdom of God.

📖 STUDY THE WORD

UNDERSTANDING THE TERMS

enmity: hostility of opposing sides.

the world: everything and everyone who is not part of the Kingdom of God.

antichrist: any demonic spirit that refuses to acknowledge Christ and opposes the truth.

Read John 15:1-10. How does Jesus describe our relationship with Him and the Father?

_____

_____

_____

_____

_____

Read Colossians 2:6-15. What does this scripture tell us to remember when we face the enemy's deception?

_____

_____

_____

_____

_____

Read 1 John 4:1-6. What does John tell us to do about opposing spirits?

_____

_____

_____

❓ THINK ABOUT IT

How does this study change how you think about yourself?

I will stay rooted deeply in Jesus.

_____

_____

_____

_____

_____

_____

_____

Be Willing to Wait as Long as it Takes
DAY 4

There is almost always a waiting period between the time we begin praying and believing about a problem and the time we see the victory over it. As time passes and the symptoms or conditions seem to be stubbornly hanging on or getting worse, the pressure will continue to build. It may become increasingly difficult to keep those doubts and questions from weakening or stealing our faith. This waiting period is the real test of what we believe, and it's where many a victory is lost. If results don't come as quickly as we think they should, we get discouraged and weary and begin to question whether it really is God's will for us. This can happen regardless of what kind of problem we're battling. When our body is in pain, or our house needs a new roof, or our marriage seems to be falling apart, it's hard to "cast all our care upon Him." Our thoughts will become questions: "Did Jesus really bear my sickness? Is God really my Source for getting a new roof? Could it be that my marriage was a mistake? Have I done something "bad" and God can't help me? Is God sending this oppression to keep me humble?"

During this waiting period is a crucial time to keep feeding the truth of the Word into our spirit. We must get the promise for the situation and plant it so firmly into our heart that we simply cannot think of it any other way or speak of it any other way than the way God says it. When we've heard from God about an answer, we must close our ears and eyes to any other thoughts and influences. We may need to turn away from the media and (kindly but firmly) keep a polite distance from well-meaning friends and relatives with opposite views. We can counter satanic thoughts by constantly reminding ourselves that God does not produce doubt, fear, accusation, or confusion. He can give us peace in the midst of the battle.

A mountain can be moved with sufficient force, but it is not likely to be moved in a day or a week. We're responsible for keeping the force of our faith applied against it and not letting up. We must believe God is at work behind the scenes, dealing with other people who may be involved and maneuvering circumstances to make our victory possible.

A child is waiting after school for his father to come get him, but it's getting late. The child's response to this problem is, "I know he will come." If you ask him why he believes this, he would tell you three basic things he knows about his father. They are so firmly established in his heart and mind that he could not easily be "talked out of" waiting indefinitely. We must develop this same childlike confidence for our own seemingly impossible situations:

"He said he would come and get me." (God always keeps his word to me.)
"He has a good car." (God has the power to do what He said He would do.)
"He would not want to disappoint me." (God loves me and wants the best for me.)

UNDERSTANDING THE TERMS
patience: endurance, calmness, courage, inner strength.

to stand: to resist an enemy force, refusing to fall or yield.

overcomers: believers who gain spiritual victory over satanic forces.

📖 STUDY THE WORD

Read Ephesians 6:10-20. Why is the word "stand" used three times in this passage?

_____

_____

_____

_____

Read Colossians 1:9-14. What is it that enables us to endure with patience and joy?

_____

_____

_____

_____

Read Hebrew 11. What was it that earned these Old Testament characters a place among these heroes of faith?

_____

_____

_____

Faith
+
patience
=
victory.

❓ THINK ABOUT IT

How does this study change the way you think about some struggle in your own life?

_____

_____

_____

_____

Praise God for the Victory
DAY 5

Praise is one of our most effective weapons in the "fight of faith." This is how Abraham was able to sustain his faith through many years while he waited for God to fulfill his promise. God's purpose was to produce and prepare a special nation from which to bring forth His Son. He chose to begin that nation with Abraham, but a son was not born to Abraham for many years. During that long wait, Abraham had to learn to trust God. Since there was no written Word to which Abraham could turn for faith, God spoke directly to him and gave him object lessons. Night after night, Abraham could look at the stars and say, "Thank you, O great Jehovah, that my descendants are as numerous as those stars." God even changed Abraham's name, so that he was called "Father of a nation" every time someone called his name. He began to praise and glorify God for a son, long before he could actually see a little boy playing in his tent. He must have had many opportunities to doubt, but he refused to consider the obvious physical facts. His body was old, and Sarah had always been barren. Yet, God had spoken, and Abraham kept his focus on his belief that God would be faithful to do what He had promised. Eventually, Abraham's doubts gave way to hope, and hope to unshakable faith when he could praise God for the victory even before the miracle came.

This must be our example if we're to begin seeing more victories. "Faith is the assurance of things hoped for." We remember to focus on the promises; we declare aloud what we believe about our Heavenly Father. As we do this, we should eventually find that we can "see" the answer in our spirit. This "knowing" brings forth gratitude and an inner peace that simply must be expressed in joyous praise. We not only declare the victory, we sing it and shout it and perhaps even dance. The enemy hates this kind of praise because it's the surest sign that our faith in the Word of Truth has defeated him. Rejoicing also helps to drown out any voices that would argue against what we believe and could weaken our faith and rob us of the victory. It must have seemed like an impossible dream to Abraham at first, but his faith grew strong AS he praised God. Praise itself will help to keep our spirit in control and our faith strong in the face of "hopeless" situations.

When we praise God for answers we cannot yet see, our thoughts may scream at us that we're speaking lies. Although the contrary evidence may be very real to our senses, we must remember that there is a higher, more powerful truth

⚷ KEY SCRIPTURE

Rejoice in the Lord always; again I will say, Rejoice. Let all men know your forbearance. The Lord is at hand. Have no anxiety about anything, but in everything by prayer and supplication with thanksgiving let your requests be made known to God.
(Phil. 4:4-6 RSV)

Therefore, we do not lose heart. Though outwardly we are wasting away, yet inwardly we are being renewed day by day. For our light and momentary troubles are achieving for us an eternal glory that far outweighs them all. So we FIX OUR EYES, not on what is seen, but on what is unseen. For what is seen is temporary, but what is unseen is eternal.
(2 Cor. 4:16-18 NIV)

All the promises of God find their Yes in him. That is why we utter the Amen through him, to the glory of God.
(2 Cor. 1:20 RSV)

They who wait for the Lord shall renew their strength, they shall mount up with wings like eagles, they shall run and not be weary, they shall walk and not faint.
(Is. 40:31 RSV)

established and operating in our spirit. We're actually praising God for a spiritual truth that transcends the evidence we can see, hear, feel, or understand. This kind of faith comes when we "trust in the Lord with all our heart and lean not to our own understanding." (Prov. 3:5 KJV)

📖 STUDY THE WORD

Read 2 Chronicles 20:1-30. How did Jehoshaphat use praise in his "impossible" situation?

_____

_____

_____

_____

_____

_____

Read Acts 16:16-34. How did Paul and Silas keep their faith strong in their "impossible" situation? What was the result?

_____

_____

_____

_____

_____

_____

❓ THINK ABOUT IT

How does this study change your thinking about praise as it relates to faith?

_____

_____

_____

_____

_____

_____

_____

_____

_____

UNDERSTANDING THE TERMS

praise: acclamation; jubilation; celebration; exultation.

sacrifice of praise: the offering of praise by deliberate choice, when there is no discernable reason for praise.

We bring the sacrifice of praise.

UNIT 8 What Are the Enemies of Faith? Part I

Insufficient Bible Study
DAY 1

Because faith is so important to our well-being, now and forevermore, and because it's a product of our spirit, we must learn how to protect it as well as nourish it. God's enemy, Satan, is our enemy also, and he's well aware that faith is a powerful force. He is also aware that we get faith by knowing, believing, and confessing the truth of God's Word. Therefore, his strategy has always been to do anything it takes to keep us ignorant, confused, weak, and quiet. We must learn to recognize these methods and know how to counteract them in order to keep our faith strong to receive God's blessings and win victories for Him.

The Word tells us the truth about Who God is, about His purposes, about the defeat of the devil, and about our authority over the devil in Jesus Christ. It tells us what Jesus has done to redeem us from the curse of sin and to provide the blessings that are ours under the Blood Covenant. If we truly want to mature in the things of God, we will study the Bible hungrily and become totally committed to believing it — not just the parts we can understand, but all of it. Because of the tremendous power in the written Word, God has deliberately hidden His truths. They are there for His children who desire to know them and choose to believe them and diligently live by them.

For many centuries, Satan tried to wipe out the Word of God altogether. When that didn't work, he tried to keep it out of the hands of believers. By leaving it to religious leaders to interpret the scripture for the people, false teachings and corrupt practices almost destroyed the Church. The history of this precious book is written in the blood of countless martyrs whose suffering has brought it to us. Since that failed, Satan is using the opposite strategy. Although the Bible is readily available almost everywhere today, too few Christians read it regularly or get much out of reading it. Satan has effectively deceived many into believing that the Bible is too difficult to understand or that it is not relevant for our problems today. Nothing could be further from the truth. Jesus promised that if we ask, the Holy Spirit will reveal its truths to us as we're able to grasp them. Instead of the dull, forbidding book it could be, the Holy Spirit will cause the Word to come alive for us and in us, if we will but study it.

KEY SCRIPTURE

The sower soweth the word. And these are they by the way side, where the word is sown; but when they have heard, Satan cometh immediately, and taketh away the word that was sown in their hearts.
(Mk. 4:14-15 KJV)

Study to shew thyself approved unto God, a workman that needeth not to be ashamed, rightly dividing the word of truth.
(2 Tim. 2:15 KJV)

Though we walk in the flesh, we do not war after the flesh. (For the weapons of our warfare are not carnal, but mighty through God to the pulling down of strong holds:) Casting down imaginations, and every high thing that exalteth itself against the knowledge of God, and bringing into captivity every thought to the obedience of Christ.
(2 Cor. 10:3-6 KJV)

Satan WILL oppose us. He hates the Word of Truth and will do whatever works for each individual to keep us from studying it, understanding it, believing it or obeying it. Not one of us is immune to his suggestions. "You're too busy now…." "You need your sleep more than you need to read the Bible." When we allow these satanic suggestions to become excuses and we neglect to seek truth from God's Word, we open our mind to deception. This leads to questioning, doubting, and speaking contrary to what God says. We must, at all cost, guard our Bible study time and build our faith on the Word of God.

📖 STUDY THE WORD

Read Mark 4:11-20. What are some of the tactics Satan uses to keep the Word from being meaningful in our lives?

_____

_____

_____

_____

Read 2 Timothy 3:13-17. According to this passage, how is Scripture profitable for us?

_____

_____

_____

_____

Read Hebrews 4:11-13. How does this passage describe the scriptures and what they can do for us?

_____

_____

_____

? THINK ABOUT IT

How does this study change the way you think about how Bible study relates to faith?

_____

_____

_____

_____

I will sow the Word in my heart.

Prayerlessness
DAY 2

Effective faith cannot survive without a personal relationship and continuous communication between our spirit and God's Spirit. Satan and the world around us will see to that. Communication is vital to any relationship, because we're created with a need for it. When we acknowledge the reality of God and want to know Him, then we realize our need to talk to Him and to hear from Him. God, in His infinite wisdom and grace, has made this possible. He speaks to us through His Word and through the Holy Spirit living within us. We speak to Him in prayer.

Prayer has far more significance than most of us can comprehend. If we truly understood the purpose of prayer and the effect it has in the spiritual realm, there would be no problem of prayerlessness in the Church. We know from the scriptures that prayer has always played a major role in the lives of God's people. In story after story, we see how God's hand did not move in behalf of Israel until someone prayed in faith. Moses "stood in the gap" for the people to keep God from destroying them in His wrath. In one of Joshua's battles to conquer the land for Israel, his prayer caused the sun to stand still until he could win the victory. Because of Daniel's fervent prayers, God sent His mightiest angel to do battle for him and the people. For some reason that we may never fully understand, God NEEDS our prayers.

Apart from prayer, there might be no Church or Gospel message going around the world today. Jesus knew the need to pray and often spent all night in prayer. He would do nothing until He had talked to the Father. All the early believers must have believed in the power of prayer, because we see it in every book of the New Testament. They knew how to talk to God and how to listen to get His directions for what they were to do in carrying out His commission.

We cannot progress further in our spiritual growth until we clear away the confusion about the purpose of prayer and learn how to pray effectively. Along with the Word, prayer is one of our most powerful weapons in spiritual warfare and, therefore, should be our first priority. Satan knows this, and he will make it his top priority to do anything that works to keep us from praying. We need to remember that prayer is not persuading God to do something. Rather, it's bringing our spirit into line with God's will. We can learn what His will is by knowing His character, by knowing His Word, and by asking Him. We speak

KEY SCRIPTURE

This is the confidence (the assurance, the [privilege of] boldness) which we have in Him: [we are sure] that if we ask anything (make any request) according to His will (in agreement with His own plan) He listens to and hears us. And if (since) we [positively] know that He listens to us in whatever we ask, we also know [with settled and absolute knowledge] that we have [granted us as our present possessions] the requests made of Him.
(1 Jn. 5:14-15 AMP)

The earnest (heartfelt, continued) prayer of a righteous man makes tremendous power available [dynamic in its working].
(Jam. 5:16b Amp)

His promises into our situation and declare our trust in Him and in His Word. Then we can make our requests known and stand in faith, confident that He hears and answers. As we mature in our spiritual growth, we must learn to be consistent and fervent in our praying. Only through prayer will we be able to keep our faith strong for the battles we face in our own lives and in the Church.

📖 STUDY THE WORD

Read Acts 6:1-4. From this scripture, what can we conclude were the top priorities of the early Church?

_____

_____

_____

_____

_____

Read Ephesians 6:10-18. How does prayer play a part in spiritual warfare?

_____

_____

_____

_____

_____

Read James 5:13-18. What kind of prayer is a "prayer of faith"?

_____

_____

_____

_____

_____

❓ THINK ABOUT IT

How does this study change the way you think about the purpose of prayer?

_____

_____

_____

_____

_____

_____

I give myself to prayer.
(Ps. 109:4b)

Pride and a Hardened Heart
DAY 3

Because of our human weakness, there will be times in all our lives, when we know what God says in His Word, but we simply refuse to be persuaded by it or to obey it. The Bible calls this a "hardened heart" or being "stiff-necked." The Israelites, throughout much of their history, could be described in this way. Despite great manifestations of God's power in their behalf and many prophetic warnings, they often refused to believe God could or would do what He had promised. Instead, they followed the counsel of their own minds and turned to their own man-made idols for help.

Despite our desire to serve God, many of us do much the same thing today. We may hear the Word again and again, but we refuse to believe what God has said in His word. Why? There may be many reasons, but one of them is that it is not popular now any more than it was in Israel. We don't like to appear strange in the eyes of friends and relatives, and the stigma of being a "religious fanatic" is something we avoid at all cost. Therefore, preferring the approval of other people instead of desiring to please God, we turn to any other source for counsel or help before we turn to God. When we do this, we spurn the blessings He has for us.

Probably the most grievous sin that Satan plants in the heart of man is pride. Pride was the sin that caused Lucifer to rebel against God. It was a major factor in Adam's rebellion. It has been the underlying cause behind much of the corruption in the history of nations and even in the history of the Church. Pride can do more to destroy our faith and our witness, not to mention our peace and joy, than we can possibly comprehend. Since not one of us is immune from the sin of pride, we must never take it lightly. Rather, we must always be on guard against this subtle intruder. Pride can masquerade under many disguises. It might appear to be merely "a competitive or aggressive personality," "self-awareness," "self-esteem," or any one of many human traits the world calls desirable.

Most of us, until we mature in this area, will go to great lengths to protect what can actually put us at enmity with God and is, therefore, one of our greatest enemies. The term "stiff-necked" may have come from a method used by ancient kings to bring a captured ruler into submission. He was forced to bend his neck and bow down low as he passed under a rod. This required him to

KEY SCRIPTURE

This people's heart has become calloused; they hardly hear with their ears, and they have closed their eyes. Otherwise they might see with their eyes, hear with their ears, understand with their hearts and turn, and I would heal them.
(Mt. 13:15 NIV)

Even many of the Jewish leaders believed him to be the Messiah but wouldn't admit it to anyone because of their fear that the Pharisees would excommunicate them from the synagogue, for they loved the praise of men more than the praise of God. .
(Jn. 12:42-43 TLB)

surrender his will to the will of his captor. Although God never wants to humiliate us, if we're not willing to see ourselves bowing in submission to God, then our heart is still hard, and we have not yet fully surrendered to His Lordship over us. Only the Holy Spirit can show us areas of pride in our life and can lead us through experiences that will cleanse it from our heart. Strong faith cannot live in a heart full of pride.

UNDERSTANDING THE TERMS

pride: the sin of an uplifted heart against God and man.

The proud: the insolent, overbearing, boastful, presumptuous.

hardness (of heart): stubbornness; obstinate refusal to obey God's known will.

📖 **STUDY THE WORD**

Read Mark 7:14-23. What does this scripture say about pride and its relationship to faith?

_____

_____

_____

_____

_____

Read Hebrews 3:7-19. How does this story illustrate the danger of pride?

_____

_____

_____

_____

_____

Read Matthew 23:1-12. What did Jesus say in the scripture about the result of pride?

_____

_____

_____

_____

My heart is as clay in the potter's hands.

? **THINK ABOUT IT**

How has this study helped you see an area of your own life where pride is a problem?

_____

_____

_____

_____

Unforgiveness and Strive
DAY 4

Jesus had much to say about holding bitterness against others in our heart. The New Testament writers recognized this as one of the greatest enemies of faith and spiritual maturity. They taught that forgiving others from the heart is absolutely necessary for faith to work in receiving God's blessings. In fact, unforgiveness is such a strong hindrance to faith that we should look in our own heart first when we seem to be unable to get answers to our prayers. Our mind and emotions must not be in control. Rather, we must "walk in the Spirit," and, by faith, allow the spiritual forces of love and longsuffering to empower us to forgive, regardless of the severity of the offense against us.

Anger, resentment, and bitterness open the door to the devil and make us vulnerable to his deception. Every person, believer and unbeliever alike, will have stressful encounters with other people; this almost always leads to strife; Satan will see to it. Having these feelings is not the problem. Dealing with them is a battle we will fight throughout our lifetime. Unforgiveness and strife weaken our faith in God and rob us of our peace and joy and victory. Jesus, throughout His ministry, taught about how serious it is to harbor unforgiveness, even when we've been treated unfairly.

The Apostle Paul must have encountered bitterness and strife among the people in every one of his churches, because he deals with it in almost every letter. He understood the ongoing struggle between our old nature and our new nature. Human nature derives a certain kind of satisfaction from holding on to resentment or getting revenge. He reminded them (and us) that anger and unforgiveness grieve the Holy Spirit and keep us from bearing the kind of fruit that pleases the Father and represents His kingdom to the World.

Paul recognized this as a battle. He gives us strategies with which to counter Satan's attacks. If they worked for Paul, they will work for us. In our relationships with other people, we no longer have to act and react out of our old nature. We just need to remember that Jesus lives in us. By deliberate choice, we can call on HIS compassion, HIS kindness, HIS patience, HIS forgiveness, or HIS grace — whatever the situation requires. The characteristics of His nature will rise up from our spirit and empower us to act as HE would act and react as HE would react. This is true spiritual maturity. It may seem unattainable this side of heaven, but it should be our all-consuming desire —

KEY SCRIPTURE

Listen to me! You can pray for anything, and if you believe, you have it; it's yours! But when you are praying, first forgive anyone you are holding a grudge against, so that your Father in heaven will forgive you your sins too.
(from Mk. 11:22-25 TLB)

Be gentle and ready to forgive; never hold grudges. Remember, the Lord forgave you so you must forgive others.
(Col. 3:13 TLB)

What I am eager for is that all the Christians there will be filled with love that comes from pure hearts, and that their minds will be clean and their faith strong.
(1 Tim. 1:5 TLB)

our ultimate quest. We will be tempted many times to give up and allow our emotions to take control. "Turning the other cheek" takes far more spiritual strength than most of us have. Overcoming the human tendency to harbor resentment is the maturing work of the Holy Spirit in the surrendered heart. It's the only way the unsaved world will be able to recognize the true followers of Jesus.

📖 STUDY THE WORD

Read Matthew 5:21-26, and 38-48. What did Jesus mean by "going the second mile"?

_____

_____

_____

_____

Read Matthew 6:9-15. What did Jesus say would be the result of unforgiveness?

_____

_____

_____

_____

Read Ephesians 4:17-32. What did Paul say we should do when we're offended?

_____

_____

_____

_____

❓ THINK ABOUT IT

How has this study helped you deal with areas of unforgiveness in your own heart?

_____

_____

_____

_____

_____

UNDERSTANDING THE TERMS

offended: displeased, indignant, resentful.

resentment: anger, animosity, bitterness, hatred.

malice: spite, ill-will.

tenderhearted: compassionate, understanding

Strife and love cannot live in the same heart.

A Sense of Unworthiness
DAY 5

An attitude of unworthiness can weaken our faith and keep us from growing spiritually or from receiving the blessings God wants us to have. Deep-seated feelings that we're unworthy or unacceptable to others and to God may have been building from childhood. Those feelings could come from the way we were taught, and they may be difficult to overcome. They could even have come from something we heard from a teacher or preacher or priest. For centuries, some churches and church leaders have added rules, regulations, and traditions to the Gospel message. In some cases, they have built a huge following of people who believe there are consequences for disobeying those rules or breaking those traditions.

Whatever may be the reason for this sense of unworthiness, it will keep us from building a strong, overcoming faith. Therefore, these feelings must be rejected. The world will call this "poor self-esteem," and specialists of all kinds will prescribe remedies to help us "come out of it." True self-esteem, however, is not a product of our own mind or a matter of "taking control" of our lives. We must base our self-worth on our position IN Jesus Christ, purified by His blood and "robed in HIS righteousness."

Some of us may find it difficult to believe God's promises of spiritual, physical, and material blessing because we're convinced that we've done too many "bad" things and could not possibly be worthy to receive anything from God. We strive to live better and to do more for the Lord, but we continually fall short of our own (or someone else's) standards of conduct. In frustration, we conclude that we should never expect a close relationship with God, and we should not expect Him to bless us. This kind of thinking is the result of Satan's deception. While a sense of unworthiness may appear to be humility, it can be a matter of either not knowing or choosing to deny the substitutionary sacrifice of Jesus Christ. The Good News is that His righteousness has been imputed to us. The blessings, then, are ours through acceptance of what HE has already done, not what WE do or don't do. We obey and serve God out of love and gratitude and because we desire to be a part of His plan.

Not one of us deserves anything from God because of what we do, and not one of us is denied by God because of what we have done in the past. Believing in the atonement of Jesus is the only thing that qualifies us for His gifts, and even

KEY SCRIPTURE

We are praying, too, that you will be filled with his mighty, glorious strength so that you can keep going no matter what happens — always full of the joy of the Lord, and always thankful to the Father who HAS MADE US FIT to share all the wonderful things that belong to those who live in the Kingdom of light. For he has rescued us out of the darkness and gloom of Satan's kingdom and brought us into the Kingdom of his dear Son, who bought our freedom with his blood and forgave us all our sins
(Col. 1:11-14 TLB)

the faith to believe is a gift from God. This is a vital spiritual truth, which the Holy Spirit wants to reveal to us in order to free us to be all that God wants us to be.

UNDERSTANDING THE TERMS
false humility: outward manifestation of modesty intended to impress others but not genuinely felt in the heart.

workmanship: that which is the result of the work of a craftsman.

📖 STUDY THE WORD

Read Ephesians 2:10. Who does Paul say we are?

_____

_____

_____

_____

_____

Read Romans 3:21-28. Paul was again reminding us of something we tend to forget easily. What was it?

_____

_____

_____

_____

Read Galatians 3:21-29. According to this scripture, what do we have to do to inherit Abraham's blessings?

_____

_____

_____

_____

_____

❓ THINK ABOUT IT

How has this study helped you deal with feelings of unworthiness?

*In Jesus
I am
much more
than
just me.*

_____

_____

_____

_____

_____

_____

_____

UNIT 9 What Are the Enemies of Faith? Part II

Double-Mindedness
DAY 1

"The world" includes every person that is not yet part of God's Kingdom, and the world never has and never will understand the ways and purposes of God. Therefore, people of the world will not understand those of us who are growing up in God's Kingdom. As believers, we need to realize this, because it will make a difference in the way we relate to other people and the way we view any situation in our life. Victorious faith absolutely depends upon our understanding this truth, for until we do, we will continue to be double minded.

Double mindedness is also called wavering. We waver when we read God's Word and want to believe what it says, but we're still wondering how it can be true, especially in the light of "worldly" knowledge. Since we have human tendencies and limitations, each of us will invariably experience this to some degree from time to time. Although it's understandable, it's still unbelief and can be an enemy of faith.

Wavering is usually the result of limited knowledge of God's ways and purposes. One of the surest signs of spiritual immaturity is wondering and questioning. We wonder, "Is this really for us today?" or "If this promise is really true, why didn't my cousin get the miracle she was claiming from God?" or "Should I even be asking God for this?" Faith is ASSURANCE, but it must be supported by the power of patience, and patience itself is fruit that grows out of our Spirit. Therefore, to overcome double-mindedness, we must keep feeding our spirit with the Word of God and steadfastly guard against any contrary thoughts.

Double-mindedness also comes from trying to walk in both worlds. Victorious faith requires total commitment to God and absolute confidence — unwavering, uncompromising, unyielding confidence — in His faithfulness. This makes communication with "the world" very difficult, because those around us will not understand us and will unwittingly say and do things that weaken our commitment and our faith. As mature believers, we must resist doubt by feeding our faith with the Word of God and boldly saying, to ourselves and others:

KEY SCRIPTURE

Let him ask in faith, nothing wavering. For he that wavereth is like a wave of the sea driven with the wind and tossed. For let not that man think that he shall receive any thing of the Lord. A double minded man is unstable in all his ways.
(Jam. 1:6-8 KJV)

Then we will no longer be like children, forever changing our minds about what we believe because someone has told us something different, or has cleverly lied to us and made the lie sound like the truth. Instead, we will lovingly follow the truth at all times — speaking truly, dealing truly, living truly — and so become more and more in every way like Christ who is the Head of his body, the Church.
(Eph. 4:14-16a TLB)

- God's Word is true and CANNOT fail. It is my final authority, and I take my stand on God's promises.
- I live by uncompromising trust in the power, wisdom and goodness of God.
- While I wait, I will be consistent, persistent, and insistent in my prayers and my confession.

Double-minded, unstable Christians with weak faith will not win the world for the Kingdom of God. The world is vainly looking for stability in all the wrong places. They need to see believers who have found stability in God and in His Word.

📖 STUDY THE WORD

Read Matthew 7:24-29. How does Jesus describe the foundation of the two houses? What do you think the "rock" represents?

_____

_____

_____

Read James 1:1-8. James wrote to believers who were suffering for their faith. What are his instructions to them (and us) about how to keep our faith strong in such trials?

_____

_____

_____

Read Psalm 112. How does the Psalmist describe a believer's heart?

_____

_____

❓ THINK ABOUT IT

How has this study helped you deal with areas of your life where you have been double-minded?

_____

_____

_____

_____

I will take my stand on the truth.

Greed and Covetousness
DAY 2

God has never been opposed to His people having possessions — even possessions beyond their actual needs. In fact, it seems from many Old Testament stories that He was lavish with His blessings for those who obeyed His laws. That was His promise under the Old Covenant — "Obey me and be blessed; go your own way and find yourself needing what only I can provide." Abraham had possessions enough to require a small army of servants to take care of them. As believers, we're heirs of all the blessings of Abraham, and under the New Covenant, we have even better promises.

Having a surplus of possessions beyond our actual needs, however, is an awesome responsibility. The things we own or want to own can become a serious enemy of our faith. The things themselves are not the problem, but the motives of our heart can quickly turn to the sin of greed and coveting. Eventually, it can lead to the idolatry of trusting in the power and position that accompany wealth, instead of trusting God. That's why God commanded, "Thou shalt not covet." It's why Jesus and the New Testament writers warn us of its dangers.

As we submit, day by day, to the teaching of the Holy Spirit, we should find that we have less and less desire for earthly possessions. Until we develop this maturity, the world and things in the world can have a strong appeal for us. The Word of God warns us about this tendency, because friendship with the world puts us at enmity with God. Therefore, we cannot expect God to bless any form of greed within us or any desire that promotes selfishness or covetousness.

Since this appeal is so subtle, how can we avoid falling into this deception? We must see it, like all other sin, for what it is — another of Satan's devices to weaken the foundation of our faith. Anything that turns our attention and devotion from God to the world will satisfy Satan's scheme. Our counter-attack, then, is a choice. Every day we must acknowledge that God owns everything — our life and everything He's provided for us while we live on earth. We must view everything we have as a stewardship, and accept the responsibility that comes with it.

When this becomes our way of thinking, and serving God becomes our way of life, the things we possess will have no power over us. We'll hold "things" so

KEY SCRIPTURE

He said unto them, Take heed, and beware of covetousness: for a man's life consisteth not in the abundance of the things which he possesseth.
(Lk. 12:15 KJV)

Keep your lives free from the love of money and be content with what you have, because God has said, "Never will I leave you; never will I forsake you."
(Heb. 13:5 NIV)

When you ask, you do not receive, because you ask with wrong motives, that you may spend what you get on your pleasures.
(Jam. 4:3 NIV)

lightly that we'll be able to let them go with a mere whisper from the Holy Spirit to our spirit. Giving back to God a tenth of what we have will be cheerful acknowledgement that all we have is His, not ours.

This is true spiritual maturity, but it doesn't come quickly or easily. Our human nature — our flesh — seeks personal comfort, pleasure, and prestige in ownership. If believers are to win the world for the Kingdom of God, we need a strong faith to trust God for all our needs. On the other hand, God needs believers who would give up everything to be a channel of His blessings to the world.

📖 STUDY THE WORD

Read Matthew 19:16-22. This is the story of the rich young ruler. What was the choice he had to make? What was the result?

_____

_____

_____

_____

Read Luke 12:13-34. What did Jesus say was the way to avoid the pitfalls of greed and covetousness?

_____

_____

_____

Read 1 Timothy 6:6-10. How does this scripture relate money and faith?

_____

_____

_____

❓ THINK ABOUT IT

How has this study changed your attitude about what you own?

_____

_____

_____

_____

_____

UNDERSTANDING THE TERMS

coveting: a strong desire for something that belongs to another person.

greed: a strong desire for more possessions than one already has or needs.

contentment: satisfaction with what one already has.

All I have is His.

Depending upon Religion or Tradition
DAY 3

"Religion" and "Christianity" are not interchangeable terms. "Religion" refers to any system of beliefs, which can include paganism and atheism. "Christianity" refers to a relationship between Jesus Christ and His followers. Religion can actually be a hindrance to the kind of faith that a lost soul needs when he turns from his sin and becomes a Christian. It can even keep a believer's faith weak and ineffective. The most religious people who heard Jesus preach were the ones who most vehemently rejected the truths He taught. God gave His people the Mosaic Law to be guidelines for their relationship with Him and with one another. By the time Jesus came to earth, the Jewish leaders had bound the people like slaves to the countless laws and traditions they had added.

Satan has skillfully used religion to keep a great part of the Church in bondage for centuries. When Bibles were rare and common citizens could not read, church leaders were the only ones who had access to the scriptures. The clergy interpreted them out of their own human understanding and forced the people to obey blindly whatever they were told to do or not do. This problem has not gone away. Even today, many Christians limit their knowledge and understanding about God to whatever they hear from a pulpit by a preacher or a priest. Because of this, many are still struggling and confused about what God wants and what their church wants.

Wherever churchgoers rely solely on the pulpit for spiritual knowledge and never question the truth of what they hear, a door opens for deception. Large congregations are being built by church groups that are willing to change their views and their customs to meet the popular demands of the changing culture — regardless of whether it agrees with God's Word.

Jesus taught that God is not impressed with even the most diligent obedience to religious rituals or to man's rules and traditions. He is interested in hearts that seek to know Him and to imitate Him, and He cares where they get their information. Believers today — perhaps more than ever before — must beware of falling prey to false teaching. What looks like piety may be empty show. What sounds like godly instruction may be meaningless human philosophy. The popularity of a church leader may come from his willingness to compromise with the world.

KEY SCRIPTURE

Understand this, that in the last days there will come (set in) perilous times of great stress and trouble [hard to deal with and hard to bear]. For people will be lovers of self and [utterly] self-centered...For [although] they hold a form of piety (true religion), they deny and reject and are strangers to the power of it...Avoid [all] such people [turn away from them].
(2 Tim. 3:1-7 AMP)

In vain do they worship me, teaching for doctrines the commandments of men.
(Mt. 15:9 RSV)

Is it possible for sincere believers to avoid such subtle traps? Indeed, we do have a way, but it requires continual vigilance and a never-ending commitment to know and obey God's Word. Jesus said the Holy Spirit would be our Guide, our Counselor, and our Teacher. He will always lead us to the cross and remind us that our righteousness is in Jesus. With His help, we can live free of legalism, tradition and compromise. Our relationship with Jesus Christ is all we need.

📖 STUDY THE WORD

Read Colossians 2:8-23. What did Paul say in this letter about keeping rules and conditions?

_____

_____

_____

_____

_____

UNDERSTANDING THE TERMS

doctrine: a principle or creed presented for acceptance and belief.

creed: an authoritative statement of religious belief.

tradition: unwritten religious precepts and customs passed down from one generation to another.

piety: reverence for God.

legalism: strict adherence to the letter of the law instead of the spirit of it.

Read Philippians 3:3-12. What did Paul say about keeping the Law?

_____

_____

_____

_____

_____

Read 2 Timothy 3:1-7. What did Paul say about people who have a "form of religion"?

_____

_____

_____

_____

❓ THINK ABOUT IT

How has this study changed your attitude about religion?

_____

_____

_____

_____

_____

*In Jesus,
I am complete.*

Fear
DAY 4

This does not refer to the natural, instinctive fear that prevents us from doing foolish acts against all sensible health and safety rules. It does not refer to the reverential fear we have toward God. It refers to the kind of fear that is based in hopelessness and helplessness. Throughout His Word, God exhorts us to fear Him, and yet there must be hundreds of "Fear not" warnings. This leads us to conclude that wherever fear of God takes the form of loving obedience to His commandments and total trust in His provisions, there is little or no need to fear anything else.

We have many examples of this in the story of the Israelites — as they crossed the Red Sea, as they wandered in the wilderness, and as they stood ready to enter the Promised Land. They were told, again and again, not to be afraid, but to trust God. When they obeyed, God always provided food, water, and protection. When they became afraid, it showed they no longer trusted Him, and He was provoked with them. The Psalmists and the Prophets wrote encouragement to Israel to trust God, even when danger was all around them. Jesus and the New Testament writers consistently tell us not to be afraid.

No one would deny that we live in a world with danger all around us. Regardless of who we are, we will have many opportunities to be afraid. It might be fear of physical harm or sickness, loss of possessions, rejection by those we love, failure, and countless other situations. Although fear takes many forms, it comes from the kingdom of darkness, and its purpose is to rob us of the peace and joy Jesus died to give us. The closer we come to the time of Jesus' return, the greater will be Satan's efforts to fill the world with fear.

Fear, then, is one of the most powerful enemies of our faith. Satan brings fear, because it is the exact opposite of faith. Where fear is present, faith is absent or weak; where faith is present, fear is absent or weak. With so much evil around us, how can we possibly come to a place of NOT being afraid every day? With so many admonitions to "Fear not!" in God's Word, there must certainly be an answer to that question, even in this evil day.

The answer lies in how we choose to react to every fearful situation that comes our way. It may be bad news, a doctor's report, frightening surroundings, or threats for our future well being. Although it may be difficult, a strong, effective,

KEY SCRIPTURE

Be strong and of a good courage, fear not, nor be afraid of them: for the LORD thy God, he it is that doth go with thee; he will not fail thee, nor forsake thee.
(Dt. 31:6 KJV)

The LORD is my light and my salvation; whom shall I fear? The LORD is the strength of my life; of whom shall I be afraid?
(Ps. 27:1 KJV)

Peace I leave with you, my peace I give unto you: not as the world giveth, give I unto you. Let not your heart be troubled, neither let it be afraid.
(Jn. 14:27 KJV)

mature faith will always respond to fear the way the Word of God teaches us to respond. We must:

- recognize the source (Satan),
- refuse to bow to it,
- confront it with the Word of God,
- boldly declare who we are and what is ours IN Christ Jesus, and
- look to the Father, knowing He is always there with us and that our future is in His hands.

📖 **Study the Word**

Read Romans 8:12-16. Paul relates fear to a spirit of bondage. What does he mean by this?

_____

_____

_____

_____

_____

Understanding the Terms

fear: (1) reverence, honor; awe. (2) terror; dread

spiritual peace: freedom from fears, agitating passions, and moral conflicts.

Read 1 John 4:16-19. How does John relate fear and love?

_____

_____

_____

_____

Read Psalm 91. What condition must we meet in order to receive God's promise of protection?

_____

_____

_____

I will fear no evil, for thou art with me.

? **Think about it**

How has this study helped you overcome some fear in your life?

_____

_____

_____

_____

_____

Wrong Confession
DAY 5

Patterns of thought and ways of expressing those thoughts begin to form in early childhood. Then, when we're adults, it's difficult to change those habits, even when we know they need to be changed. We will not be able to use our faith effectively beyond what we're able to believe in our heart and confess to with our words. Therefore, one of the most prevalent enemies of our faith can be the remarks that come from our own lips. This principle should not be difficult for us to grasp, for we use it every day. We settle business transactions with statements, both verbal and written. We make a marriage commitment by declaring, "I do," and "I will." Just as surely, we often "sign up for" (accept) whatever Satan tries to give us, simply by agreeing with him that we "have it."

If, on the other hand, we read the Word of God and believe it's true, we can use the same principle and verbally claim all the promises of God that belong to us. Jesus taught that our words are open declarations of what we're thinking and are undeniable indications of what we believe in our heart. When those declarations are opposed to the promises of God, then we're exposing the doubts and fears that have not yet been put to rest. Every one of us who has received salvation had to come by faith (believing in our heart) and confession (saying aloud) that we accept Jesus as our personal Redeemer. We receive all the other promises in the same way.

When God wanted the Hebrew fathers to teach the commandments to their children, He instructed them to write them on their doorposts and then quote them aloud every time they came in or went out. We can do this simple thing for ourselves. We can personalize the promises we're claiming, write them, and post them where we can see them and speak them aloud until they become what we firmly believe.

The children of God who are living in the greatest freedom are the childlike ones who take God at His simple Word and trust Him to do exactly what He said. We will seldom hear a mature believer express doubt or fear in his conversation. Instead, we're likely to hear him quoting promises to affirm what he believes in his heart.

We must learn to listen to our own conversation and identify the doubt-filled remarks we make that weaken our faith. We can ask the Holy Spirit to help us

KEY SCRIPTURE

If you confess with your mouth, "Jesus is Lord," and believe in your heart that God raised him from the dead, you will be saved. For it is with your heart that you believe and are justified, and it is with your mouth that you confess and are saved.
(Rom.10:9-10 NIV)

Let the words of my mouth, and the meditation of my heart, be acceptable in thy sight, O LORD my strength, and my redeemer.
(Ps. 19:14 KJV)

"hear" our own words and remind us when we speak in opposition to God's Word. He can help us develop positive confessions. If we find that we simply cannot vocally and publicly claim something God has promised, it's a sure sign that we don't really believe it yet. Our faith is weak and ineffective. We must feed those promises into our spirit until we can declare boldly and with absolute ASSURANCE, that they are ours.

📖 STUDY THE WORD

Read Matthew 15:10-20. According to this passage, from where do evil thoughts come?

_____

_____

_____

_____

_____

Read James 3:3-12. What are some of the things that result from words we speak?

_____

_____

_____

_____

_____

Read Deuteronomy 6:4-9. How were the Hebrew fathers instructed to teach there children?

_____

_____

_____

I will not think doubt-filled thoughts or speak doubt-filled words.

❓ THINK ABOUT IT

How has this study helped you begin to listen to your own words?

_____

_____

_____

_____

_____

UNIT 10 Where Am I Now in My Spiritual Growth?

Who Is Ruling My Life?
DAY 1

Spiritual maturity is what each of us should be seeking, from the time we're born again and become children of God. We should never be content to stay where we are in our spiritual development. Yet, how can we determine whether we are still at the infant stage or are making significant progress? Since our ultimate goal is to grow up into Christ, we can know how close we are to that goal by looking at our conduct and listening to our conversation. We can ask ourselves questions to help us recognize areas of weakness, and then ask the Holy Spirit to show us how to grow stronger in those areas.

We must, at all times, know Who is on the throne of our life. The sincere desire of our heart must be to reach the place in our spiritual growth where we live to please God and God only. When He literally becomes the motivating factor for everything we do, then all the other areas of our life will fall into their proper places. Even while we still exist on this planet and obey the laws of a nation, our true citizenship is in the Kingdom of God. We live by Kingdom principles, obey Kingdom laws, and acknowledge allegiance to the King of Glory.

Since this Kingdom is an invisible realm, we can expect an on-going conflict between it and the visible realm in which we live. The sinful tendencies of our human nature are constantly fighting to put SELF on the throne. Therefore, we must be on guard against any indication that we may be yielding to this temptation. We can ask the Holy Spirit to help us "hear" SELF in our thoughts and our responses to everyday situations. If we listen with "ears that hear," we will learn to recognize thoughts and remarks that are characteristic of self-defense, self-promotion, self-justification, self-righteousness, self-indulgence, and self-dependency. Each one indicates an area where we have not yet fully surrendered.

Surrender! That is the key that opens the door to the Kingdom of Heaven, and that's the response that puts us on our face before the King. We must surrender fully, and we must surrender daily to the work of the Holy Spirit. This will be His work in us until we accept God's love for us and allow Him to be "God" to us. We must acknowledge His power (ability to help us), His wisdom (to know how to help us), and His faithfulness (to keep His promises). We must realize

KEY SCRIPTURE

Blessed are the poor in spirit; for theirs is the kingdom of heaven.
(Mt. 5:3 NKJV)

Thy kingdom come. Thy will be done in earth, as it is in heaven....For Thine is the kingdom, and the power, and the glory forever. Amen
(Mt. 6:10, 13 KJV)

Our citizenship is in heaven, from which we also eagerly wait for the Savior, the Lord Jesus Christ.
(Phil. 3:20 NKJV)

that anything less than total dependency is a form of rebellion, and rebellion is SELF-rule.

How can any of us expect to keep SELF off the throne and stay surrendered to His Lordship over us? While we may not realize the fullest possibility of this during our lifetime, it should always be the desire of our heart. We should never stop seeking HIM and the joy of His presence. Jesus promised, "Blessed are the pure in heart, for they shall see God."

📖 **STUDY THE WORD**

Read Matthew 5:2-12. How does this list of Beatitudes relate to who is ruling our life?

_____

_____

_____

Read Matthew 6:5-15. How can praying the Lord's Prayer help us keep God on the throne of our life?

_____

_____

_____

_____

Read Philippians 4:7-16. What did Paul say in this passage that lets us know who ruled his life?

_____

_____

_____

_____

? **THINK ABOUT IT**

How has this study helped you determine who is actually on the throne of your life?

I live to serve the King of Glory.

_____

_____

_____

_____

How Steadfast Am I in Times of Trial?
DAY 2

Any child of God who makes an all-out commitment to turn away from the enticements of this world and focus on becoming like Jesus WILL meet with opposition. Persecution did not cease with the believers of the first century. It WILL come in one form or another. In some places today, people still endure physical suffering, loss of property or jobs or even families. Sometimes persecution takes the form of rejection. When friends or family members turn their backs on the one who has become "a new creation in Christ," the emotional pain can be almost unbearable.

Trials may not always come in the form of persecution. They could be any kind of distressing situation, such as sickness, infirmity, loss of a loved one, financial need, or inability to overcome a destructive habit. Not one of us is going to escape stressful problems, whatever they may be. Sometimes it seems we have more problems after we become committed to following Jesus than we had when we were walking in the world.

Since we can expect trials to come, we must learn how to deal with them so that, instead of being defeated by them, we can learn from them and be victorious over them. Jesus gave us an important principle to remember, and He was the perfect example of that principle. He said we should look upon our life in this world as temporary and live for the eternal life to come. After Jesus left the apostles, they understood what He meant, for all of them suffered terrible persecution and eventually died painful deaths. Yet, they lived seemingly without fear or concern for their own well being.

The New Testament letters were written to encourage and strengthen believers while they were going through trials. These letters can be a source of comfort to us during times of trial, and we can learn from them. Trials will test the strength of our faith and teach us patience and endurance. Therefore, during any test, we must remember all the truths we've learned about who we are in Jesus and what He has done for us. Evil men will continue to reject the cross, and their corrupt deeds will become even worse, but we can set an example before them. We can respect authority, live as peacemakers, and take our share of suffering as ambassadors for Christ.

KEY SCRIPTURE

After you have suffered a little while, the God of all grace [Who imparts all blessing and favor], Who has called you to His [own] eternal glory in Christ Jesus, will Himself complete and make you what you ought to be, establish and ground you securely, and strengthen, and settle you.
(1 Pet. 5:10 AMP)

Yea, and all that will live godly in Christ Jesus shall suffer persecution.
(2 Tim. 3:12 NIV)

Blessed is the man who perseveres under trial, because when he has stood the test, he will receive the crown of life that God has promised to those who love Him.
(Jam. 1:12 NIV)

What should be our attitude toward our persecutors? If we sincerely want to develop the spiritual maturity we seek, we will follow Jesus' example. We must refuse to retaliate or threaten. Then we must forgive the offenders and pray that God will bless them, regardless of the severity of the suffering. Like Jesus, we can trust God to give us power to endure whatever the trial may be and to bring us through it to a victory that will bring Him glory and honor. He promised that He would "never leave us nor forsake us."

📖 STUDY THE WORD

Read 2 Timothy 3:10-14. Paul suffered mightily for his faith. What did he tell Timothy about facing trials?

_____

_____

_____

_____

_____

UNDERSTANDING THE TERMS

trials: events in a believer's life that test the strength of his faith.

tribulations: severe troubles that produce pain and suffering.

Read 1 Peter 2:9-25. How does Peter tell us to view suffering?

_____

_____

_____

_____

Read 1 Peter 4:1-19. In light of this scripture, how should we deal with trials and suffering today?

_____

_____

_____

_____

❓ **THINK ABOUT IT**

How has this study helped you face some trial in your own life?

_____

_____

_____

_____

_____

The trying of our faith produces patience.

(Jam. 1:3)

Do I Know How to Do Spiritual Warfare?
DAY 3

"Spiritual warfare" is a term that is relatively new to many Christians, and any mention of fighting may seem out of place for followers of Christ. As long as we live on this earth, however, we are in a very real conflict, and we deal with it every day, whether we recognize it as such or not. When Lucifer was cast out of the heavenly realm, he fell to earth, bringing a host of his followers with him. They operate here as Satan and demonic spirits — well organized and with an evil agenda to oppose God and thwart His plans and purposes. Jesus defeated Satan and took away all his authority over the earth and those who accept Jesus as Savior.

Why, then, is Satan still here, and why must we continue to deal with him at all? Satan was defeated, but he has not gone away. God wants US to learn how to withstand Satan and bring down strongholds. He wants US to bring His light into the dark places of this world and set captives free with the Good News of salvation in Jesus Christ. He wants His Church, His Body on earth, to learn how to "rule and reign with Him." Instead of remaining weak and ineffective, the Church must boldly take the offensive against satanic powers.

Fortunately, as more believers learn to live in the power of the Holy Spirit, the situation is beginning to change. Only He can teach us what we need to know if we're to be effective in spiritual warfare. He will teach us that we do have authority over the principalities and powers of darkness, and He will give us boldness to use that authority. The Holy Spirit will help us recognize areas in our life where Satan brings misery and then show us how to exercise our Covenant rights to get the victory. We must no longer cringe in fear of Satan's attacks or submit to his attempts to steal our peace and joy. The Holy Spirit is teaching us, God's army on earth, how to use all the weapons He has given us to resist every attempt of the enemy to destroy the Church.

Jesus came to give us life, freedom, joy, and peace. ANYTHING that comes to steal any part of that from us, in any area of our life, is not of God. We do not have to accept it, even if it is a mere thought that crosses our mind. Satan cannot give us anything or take anything from us without first convincing us that he can do so. That's why we must recognize any negative thoughts, such as fear, depression, worry, or self-pity as lies of the enemy. We "cast down these wicked

KEY SCRIPTURE

God has not given us a spirit of fear, but of power and of love and of a sound mind.
(2 Tim. 1:7 NKJV)

Our struggle is not against flesh and blood, but against the rulers, against the authorities, against the powers of this dark world and against the spiritual forces of evil in the heavenly realms.
(Eph. 6:12 NIV)

imaginations" and wipe them out of our minds by deliberately replacing them with the truth of God's Word.

While we live on earth, it will not be possible to live entirely free of satanic attack. We can, however, live completely free of the fear of them, because we know how to recognize them and how to resist them. We have weapons that are far more powerful than anything Satan can use. We have the authority to use the name of Jesus; we're living under the Blood Covenant; and we have the Word of God. Our responsibility is to use them.

📖 **STUDY THE WORD**
Read 1 Peter 5:6-10. How does Peter tell us to deal with the devil?

_____

_____

_____

_____

UNDERSTANDING THE TERMS
principalities: evil beings that exercise power in the kingdom of darkness.

Read Ephesians 6:10-18. Why did Paul say we need the armor of God?

_____

stronghold: like a fortress, it holds control over an area.

_____

_____

withstand: resist with power and determination.

_____

Read 2 Corinthians 10:1-6. How does this describe the weapons of our warfare?

_____

_____

_____

_____

❓ THINK ABOUT IT
How has this study helped you understand satanic strategy?

_____

I refuse to bow to the rulers of darkness.

_____

_____

_____

_____

_____

Is My Life a Model of Holiness?
DAY 4

"Holiness" is a term that has been almost lost to the Church for decades. Somehow, with the "new morality" and the so-called "freedom" introduced by the entertainment media, the idea of holiness became confused with false piety and a fanatical adherence to prudish customs. As Christians, we may sometimes find our conscience wavering between what seems to be "acceptable" conduct and what the scriptures call "holiness." Some people take an extreme view of holiness and literally separate themselves from the world and anything that might be a temptation. Some people set strict standards of conduct for themselves and then use those standards to judge the spiritual maturity of everyone else.

True "holiness" describes a lifestyle that separates the believer from the world and consecrates him to God's service. His life is committed to purity — body, mind, soul and spirit. He is willing to submit to whatever needs to be done to help him "crucify the flesh" or "put off the old man" until his conduct becomes pleasing to God.

If we want to know where we are in our spiritual growth, we can look at our conduct and our lifestyle in the light of the models of holiness we find in the New Testament. Every one of the apostles lived a separated, consecrated life that must have pleased God. Before Calvary and Pentecost, however, their conduct and their conversation show them to be anything but consecrated and pure. What happened to transform these men into models of holiness?

Believers in the early Church must have struggled with the problem of holiness just as we do, because most of the letters to the churches deal with it. We can study these letters and learn from them, because what they teach applies to every believer today. They never speak of holiness lightly, as if it's a virtue only a few can hope to attain. Rather, they remind us that we serve a holy God, who expects us to become "holy, as He is holy." There is no longer any place in our life for the evil conduct that characterizes the lifestyle of those outside the Kingdom of God. Anger, lying, stealing, corrupt and evil speaking, drunkenness, sexual immorality — all of these contaminate our own life and the life of the Church.

⚷ KEY SCRIPTURE

Therefore, having these promises, beloved, let us cleanse ourselves from all filthiness of the flesh and spirit, perfecting holiness in the fear of God.
(2 Cor. 7:1 NKJV)

Pursue peace with all people and holiness, without which no one will see the Lord.
(Heb. 12:15 NKJV)

As the One Who called you is holy, you yourselves also be holy in all your conduct and manner of living.
(1 Pet. 1:15 AMP)

What can we do to attain holiness and then remain holy? We must remember who we are in Christ Jesus. We have been "raised with Christ" out of the corruption that once characterized our old life. By deliberate choice, we must consider ourselves dead to our old ways and set our minds on higher, eternal things. When living for Jesus becomes the ultimate goal of our life, questions about what is and is not "acceptable" conduct seem foolish. We will never again be satisfied until everything we do and say pleases the Father — and then our life will be a model of holiness

UNDERSTANDING THE TERMS
holiness: separation from sin; hearty obedience.

consecrated: dedicated to the service of God.

sanctified: purified and set apart for God.

separation: set apart for a specific purpose.

chastening: punishment for the purpose of removing sin.

📖 **STUDY THE WORD**

Read 2 Corinthians 6:1-7:1. In this scripture Paul wrote, "Come out from among them and be separate." What did he mean?

_____

_____

_____

_____

Read Ephesians 4:17-5:21. List some of the practices that are characteristic of the "old man." What does Paul say we should do with them?

_____

_____

_____

_____

Read Colossians 3:1-11. According to this scripture, what should we do to remain holy?

_____

_____

_____

? **THINK ABOUT IT**

How has this study helped evaluate your own conduct and lifestyle?

_____

_____

_____

_____

Without holiness, no one will see the Lord.
(Heb. 12:14)

Am I Abiding in Christ?
DAY 5

We're all on a spiritual journey, and we would like to know where we are and how close we are to our destination. To help us determine this, we must know Who is ruling our life, whether we can remain steadfast in times of trial, and whether we know how to do spiritual warfare. Then we must look at how we live day by day and know that our lifestyle is a model of holiness. All of these are important areas of spiritual growth, and most of us will know in our spirit approximately where we are in each of them — how far we've come and how much is still ahead of us. We must answer one more question that is, perhaps, the most revealing of all. Am I abiding IN Christ? Before we try to answer it, we should understand that there is a much deeper meaning imbedded in the question than most of us can grasp without divine revelation.

When Jesus talked to His disciples in the Upper Room on the night before His crucifixion, He gave them the key to every spiritual blessing we could hope for on earth. Again and again, He used the phrase "abide in." Since "abide" means "to live," Jesus is saying, "Live in me. Let my words live in you. Let me live in you." We may have read that phrase many times, but likely, we've missed the most important word of all. Jesus wants us to live IN Him, just as He lives IN the Father, and the Father lives IN Him. This is a spiritual concept that only the Holy Spirit can reveal to us, and it may take a lifetime to grasp the full revelation of it. With each bit of revelation, however, we will grow up a little more.

Jesus tried to make it easier for us to understand. He said it was like a vine and its branches. He is the vine, giving life to the branches. We are the branches, attached so firmly to the vine that we draw our very life from Him. We bear fruit when that life is flowing freely. Everything that hinders that life-flow must be pruned away so that we will produce more and better fruit. This is what "abiding in Him" means for us.

Understanding this dramatically changes the way we think about Jesus and our relationship to Him. Our quest is no longer just a search for knowledge about Jesus, although that is a necessary part of it. It is no longer an attempt to live LIKE Jesus, although that is what we want. It is not even striving to please Him, although we certainly will. We no longer see Him walking along by our side. Rather, we see our very own personal life, with all its weaknesses and imperfections, actually IN Jesus Christ, our Lord and our Savior. We are

---

KEY SCRIPTURE

God is love, and he who abides in love abides in God, and God in him.
(1 Jn. 4:16b AMP)

Abide in me, and I in you. As the branch cannot bear fruit by itself, unless it abides in the vine, neither can you, unless you abide in me.
(Jn. 15:4 RSV)

If you keep my commandments, you will abide in My love, just as I have kept My Father's commandments and abide in his love. These things I have spoken to you, that my joy may remain in you, and that your joy may be full.
(Jn. 15:10-11 NKJV)

becoming part of Him and all that He is. We see our little life so blended with His life that we easily sense His thoughts and know that He senses ours.

When we come to this place, everything in life takes on new meaning, new purpose, and new excitement. We will know with assurance where we are in our quest for spiritual maturity. We are growing up INTO Christ.

📖 STUDY THE WORD

Read John 15:1-17. According to this scripture, what does it take to "abide in" Jesus?

_____
_____
_____
_____
_____

Read Colossians 2:1-11. What does Paul say that we have "IN Him." How we can remain "IN Him"?

_____
_____
_____
_____

UNDERSTANDING THE TERMS
abide: to live in; remain in permanently.

Read Ephesians 3:14-21. If possible, read this from several translations. If we pray this as our personal prayer, what are we asking from God?

_____
_____
_____
_____

❓ THINK ABOUT IT

How has this study helped you understand what it means to abide in Christ?

_____
_____
_____
_____
_____

I am growing up INTO Christ.

Closing Session

For the past several weeks, we have been on a quest for spiritual maturity. We increased or reinforced our knowledge and understanding of God and His ways and purposes. We have a firmer grasp on some important truths about Jesus. We understand why He came to earth and what he did to rescue us from the curse of sin, reconcile us to the Father, and make us qualified to be children of God. We know some basic principles to strengthen our faith and keep us steadfast while we fulfill the commission He left for us.

Our studies have given us many opportunities to search the Word of God for answers, and we should appreciate more than ever before the divine power that is in it for us. We began the studies with a hunger to know the truths that are hidden there, and the Holy Spirit has been faithful to reveal them to us as we opened our hearts to receive them. We know we must choose to believe it, receive it into our spirit, and allow it to transform us from the inside.

Even more importantly, we have learned what it means to abide IN Christ and to reflect Him and all He is through the life we live. We desire, more than ever, to show HIM to the world around us. Every day is becoming an exciting adventure as we give Him complete control of our life and all we have. We're learning how to recognize and obey the voice of the Holy Spirit — our Teacher, our Helper, and our Comforter — as we live through every experience. We're learning that nothing else is more vital to our spiritual progress than the love that is growing in us out of the heart of the One Who lives in us. God sent Jesus to reveal His love TO the world. Now the world is waiting to see His love IN us — mature believers, living victoriously in a world full of evil.

Jesus taught that what we speak is evidence of whatever is in our heart in abundance. Therefore, we're learning to listen to our own thoughts and our own words. This is especially true in our responses to other people — and it's these responses that are the true test of our spiritual progress. We must recognize any attempt of the enemy to lead us back into the sinful ways of our "old man." Fear, envy, resentment, unforgiveness, bitterness, anger, doubt, discouragement, self-pity, worry, greed, selfishness, and self-sufficiency — all can be detected in our responses to others and to situations that arise. Our life is a never-ending series of choices and the consequences of those choices. We are responsible for rejecting negative thoughts and replacing them with God's promises. Furthermore, we must never allow ourselves to judge the spiritual progress of fellow Christians, and we must never submit to guilt and condemnation about our own progress.

While we find satisfaction in the progress we've made during this program, we must never be content to remain where we are. The quest is not the destination. There is always more to learn, and the Holy Spirit is always ready to help us learn it, "until finally we all believe alike about our Savior…and all BECOME FULL-GROWN in the Lord — yes, to the point of being FILLED FULL with Christ."

EVALUATION OF PERSONAL PROGRESS

What were the weakest areas of my spiritual life when I began this quest?

_____
_____
_____
_____
_____
_____
_____

In what ways am I stronger in these areas now?

_____
_____
_____
_____
_____
_____
_____

How has my relationship with God changed?

_____
_____
_____
_____
_____
_____

How has my relationship with other people changed?

_____

_____

_____

_____

_____

_____

What is now the motivating focus of my life?

_____

_____

_____

_____

_____

_____

What will I do to continue my quest for spiritual maturity?

_____

_____

_____

_____

_____

_____

_____

SUGGESTIONS FOR GROUP LEADERS

If you have accepted the challenge of leading this Bible study, then you have entered into what should be an important 10 to 12 weeks in your own life as well as in the lives of others. This program is a quest for spiritual maturity. Those who have joined the study group are committing themselves to considerable time and effort to gain what they feel they need in their spiritual life. Therefore, they'll be looking to you to help them make it a worthwhile pursuit. While it is an awesome responsibility, the rewards for you, as leader, could more than repay you for your diligence and dedication.

Your priorities

Throughout this program, your ultimate goal will be to help each member of your group reach a higher level of spiritual maturity. This must be the goal for each member, and it must be your own personal goal. Remind yourself constantly that this — not the program itself — is the emphasis. The daily studies your members will do at home during the week are merely a beginning place. The discussions at the group meetings will be successful only if they encourage your members to lay aside their preconceived ideas, doctrines and traditions and focus on becoming one with Jesus Christ. As you and your members grow up into Christ, you should find yourselves thinking like Jesus, acting like Jesus, and reacting like Jesus in your day-by-day experiences and relationships.

Your schedule

The study group will meet once a week. It could be a Sunday morning, Sunday evening or mid-week service. It could be a group meeting in a home setting. For an effective discussion, allow from an hour to an hour and a half for each meeting. Allow more time if you include worship and ministry. This program includes 10 units, an important Introductory Session and an optional Closing Session.

Your preparations

The actual discussion time is limited. Do whatever you can to save that time for Bible study and for encouragement.

- Keep records. Prepare a list of your members with addresses and phone numbers. You may want to keep an attendance roll.

- Make the meeting place as inviting as possible. Place chairs in a circle so that each member can see the faces of all the other members.
- Complete each study yourself, for you are a member of the group.

Respond to the Bible study questions before you look at the suggested answers in the "Helps" section. Record your own thoughts about application for your own life.

Your members' preparations

Each member will have a copy of The Quest. After the Introductory Session, each member will complete the five daily studies in Unit 1 at home during the following week. They will read the scriptures and answer the questions about them. Then, they will express how they can apply what they've learned to their own life situations. When the group meets after each week of study, ask members to discuss their responses to the daily studies of the previous week. Then, ask for volunteers to express how they will apply what they've learned. No member should, at any time, feel pressured to do so.

Your procedure

As in most group meetings, your group will likely develop a procedural pattern of its own, depending upon the personalities of the members and your guidance as the leader. Most meetings, however, will include the following elements in this tentative order:
- About 5 minutes of greeting and record keeping.
- Opening prayer. You may pray or call on someone else. It can also be one of the foundation prayers prayed in unison.
- Discuss the studies from the previous week. For best results, discuss them in the order they appear.
- Call for several members to give their responses to the scripture studies. Avoid embarrassing shy persons, but be aware of persons who dominate discussion.
- After discussing as many scriptures as time allows, ask members to tell how the study in this unit changes their thinking and how it will affect them spiritually.
- Close the meeting with prayer.
- After the meeting, make a personal evaluation. Are the members of your group excited about what they're learning? Did each member participate? Are all of them showing signs of spiritual growth in their responses to the lessons and to one another?

SUGGESTED ANSWERS TO BIBLE STUDIES

UNIT 1 Who Is God to Me?

DAY 1 — What Is God Like?

Psalm 19:1-6, when read with **Romans 1:18-20,** shows us two ways that God reveals Himself to man. One is through His creation another is through His inspired Word.

1 Corinthians 8:3-6. Paul explains that idols made by man's own hands are absolutely nothing. Anything that might be called a god is demonic. There is only one true God.

DAY 2—What Is Man Like?

John 3:1-12. Jesus told Nicodemus that "unless one is born of water and the Spirit, he cannot enter the Kingdom of God. That which is born of flesh is flesh; that which is born of the Spirit is spirit." This tells us there is a significant difference between our spirit and our soul (our mind, will and emotions.)

Psalm 8. Compared to the greatness of God, man is very small. Yet, as the ultimate life form in all of creation, he's very significant in the eyes of God.

DAY 3 — How Does God Want to Relate to Us?

1 John. The dominant theme of this letter is love — God's love for us and our responding love for Him. This love will be evident in our love for our fellow believers.

John 4:1-26. By speaking to the woman at the well, Jesus demonstrated that God's love transcends

- social justice, because she was a woman, considered inferior to men.
- age-old racial hatreds. Jews were not supposed to have anything to do with Samaritans.
- even the most blatant sins. This was an immoral woman.

DAY 4 — How Does God Want Us to Relate to Him?

Colossians 1:9-10. Paul wants Christians to know God, because knowing Him means to want to please Him, and to please Him, we will devote ourselves to walking worthy of Him.

John 17:17-26. Jesus prayed that believers might all be one, in the same way that He was one with the Father. This is how the world would know that the Father had sent the Son, and this would prove His love to them.

Jeremiah 9:23-24. We are NOT to boast about our wisdom, might or riches. God is pleased when we glory in understanding and knowing HIM and acknowledging His lovingkindness, judgment and righteousness.

DAY 5—How Does God Want Us to Relate to Other People?

John 13:33-35. Jesus gave a new commandment, "Love one another as I have loved you."

1 Corinthians 13. Love will be patient and kind. It will not be jealous or boastful or insist on its own way. Love will not rejoice at wrong, but will rejoice at right. Love will not hold grudges, but will bear whatever others may say or do. It will look for the best in others.

UNIT 2 What Was Jesus' Mission?

DAY 1 — Who Was Jesus Christ?

Mark 1:9-11 and **Matthew 3:13-17**. Jesus told John that He must be baptized "to fulfill all righteousness." By this He was affirming John's ministry and His own submission to God's call upon His life. He was not anointed with oil because that ritual was for cleansing from sin, and He had never sinned.

2 Peter 3:14-18. Peter tells us that the best way to avoid deception and false teaching is to "grow in the knowledge of our Lord Jesus Christ."

John 1:1-14. Jesus is the Word made flesh. He came to His own, but His own did not receive Him. Those who do receive Him become children of God, born of God.

DAY 2 — Why Did He Come to Earth?

Romans 5:1-21. By the one man Adam, came sin and death, judgment, many sinners, and abounding sin. By the one man Jesus, came grace and life, justification, many righteous, abounding grace, and freedom from the curse of sin.

Colossians 1:9-23. God's purpose in sending Jesus to earth was to reconcile us to Himself.

Romans 8:18-23. Creation itself will no longer be subject to decay.

DAY 3 — Why Was the Virgin Birth Necessary?

Matthew 1:18-25. The Apostle wanted Jewish Christians to believe that Jesus was truly the Son of God, born of a Virgin according to prophecy. The angel Gabriel told Joseph not to be afraid, because the child she would bear was conceived of the Holy Spirit and was the Son of God.

Luke 1:26-38. Gabriel gave Mary information about her cousin Elizabeth, who was miraculously carrying a child in her old age. This was a miracle that she could confirm, and it assured her that her own child truly was the Son of God as the angel had said.

Isaiah 7:10-14. Both Matthew and Luke recorded the event that fulfilled Isaiah's prophecy.

DAY 4 — Why Was a Sinless Life Necessary?

Matthew 26. Jesus could have refused what lay before Him. Would he become sin and break His fellowship with the Father? He knew that if He did, He would be denying the will of God.

Luke 6:1-11. Man's rules and regulations may seem to be desirable and worthy, but they may actually be a form of bondage. This is especially true if they subtly become a requirement for salvation.

DAY 5 — Why Was Calvary Necessary?

Psalm 103:1-18. God provides a way for His people to be saved (spiritually) from hell; to be healed (physically) from sickness and disease; and to be free (mentally and emotionally) from hopelessness, despair, and oppression. Under the Old Covenant, the condition was the keeping of the law. Under the New Covenant, the condition is faith and love.

Isaiah 53:4-12. Jesus bore OUR grief and sorrows; He was wounded for OUR transgressions; He was bruised for OUR iniquities; the chastisement for OUR peace was upon Him; with His stripes WE are healed; the Lord laid on him the iniquity of all of US.

Romans 8:1-11. Paul tells us that we must be IN Christ and not walk according to the flesh but according to the Spirit.

UNIT 3 What Was Jesus' Triumph?

DAY 1 — What Does His Resurrection Mean to Us?

Romans 6:1-12. Water baptism symbolizes the burial and resurrection that take place in the spirit of a person who accepts Jesus Christ as his personal Savior. It is significant to the individual as an outward sign that he is a "new creation," born again and now part of God's Kindgom.

2 Corinthians 5:14-21. This scripture reassures us that we are completely reconciled to the Father.

Philippians 3:7-11. Paul had made "knowing Jesus" the main goal of his life. The pursuit had led him to the revelation of what belongs to us when we're "raised with Christ."

DAY 2 — How Does His Triumph Help the Sinner?

Colossians 1:9-23. Paul declares that Jesus died in our place. Our part is to be fully convinced of this truth. Then, we're to stand in it, strong in the Lord, and never shift from trusting Him to save us spiritually, emotionally, and mentally.

2 Corinthians 5:14-21 and **Colossians 2:9-15**. Paul assures us that our redemption is complete in Jesus Christ. Nothing more needs to be done to assure our inheritance in Him.

DAY 3 — What Does the Blood Covenant Mean to Us?

Exodus 24:4-8. Moses, acting as mediator between God and the people, confirmed the covenant under which they would live for centuries. The blood sprinkled on the altar denoted God's forgiveness of their sins. The blood sprinkled on the people symbolized their commitment to God.

Jeremiah 31:31-34. Jeremiah prophesied about a New Covenant that would be written in their hearts.

Hebrews 8:6-13. This scripture quotes the prophecy from Jeremiah about a New

Covenant, which makes the first one obsolete.

DAY 4 — Where Is Jesus Now?

Hebrews 5:1-10. Jesus was anointed and approved by God, and He was far superior to Melchizedek, who was considered superior to all the Levitical priests. He had no need to offer sacrifices for His own sins, because He was without sin.

Hebrews 8:1-6. He is sitting at the right hand of the throne of God, mediating a covenant that is superior in every way to the old one. This one is founded on even greater promises.

Matthew 28:16-20 and Mark 16:14-20. Jesus asked His followers to take the Gospel message into the world, teaching, preaching, baptizing and healing — all in the authority of His name. He promised that He would be with them and would confirm His Word with salvations, healings, and other miracles.

DAY 5 — Where Do We Fit in God's Agenda?

Matthew 19:16-22. The rich young ruler chose to hold on to the "security" of his wealth instead of receiving what Jesus offered him.

2 Corinthians 5. Paul reminds us that we should no longer live for our own purposes but as ambassadors for Christ.

Colossians 1:9-29. Paul reveals to us that God's purpose for us has always been the same — Christ, the Anointed One, living in us.

Philippians 1:9-11. Paul consistently gave this message to all the churches about what God wants them to be doing while they wait for Christ's return. They're to bear the fruit of righteousness.

UNIT 4 Who is the Holy Spirit to Me?

DAY 1 — Why Did the Holy Spirit Come?

Psalm 51:10-12. David repented of the sin he had committed and asked God to restore his joy and not to take the Holy Spirit from him.

Luke 4:14-21. After Jesus had read the prophecy from Isaiah, He announced that the One standing before them was the fulfillment of that prophecy.

Acts 1:1-8; 2:1-4. Jesus did not want his followers to begin trying to minister in their own abilities. He sent the Holy Spirit to give them supernatural power and ability.

John 20:19-23. Jesus breathed on them and instructed them to receive the Holy Spirit.

DAY 2 — Why Is He Important to the Church?

Acts 13:1-4. The Church leaders had been praying and fasting when they received instructions from the Holy Spirit to send Paul and Barnabas on the first missionary trip.

Acts 10:19-20, 44-48. He gave Peter a vision of clean and unclean animals and declared them all "clean." Then he sent Peter to preach to a family of Gentiles, and they received salvation and the gift of the Holy Spirit.

Ephesians 4:1-13. These gifts were leaders for the Church: apostles, prophets, evangelists, pastors, and teachers.

DAY 3 — How Does He Help Us?

Luke 11:5-13. Jesus taught that the Heavenly Father will not give a useless gift to His children when they ask Him for the gift of the Holy Spirit.

Acts 2:37-39. Peter said the Holy Spirit is given as a gift to those who repent and are baptized.

John 16:1-16. Jesus told His disciples that the Holy Spirit would convict unbelievers of sin and the certainty of judgment. He would remind believers of what is ours in Jesus and bring glory to Jesus.

DAY 4 — How Do We Walk in the Spirit?

Romans 8:1-14. The mind controlled by the flesh leads to sin and all the miseries associated with death, both here and hereafter. The mind controlled by the Spirit is life and soul peace, now and forever.

Galatians 5:16-26. Those who live according to the flesh, or their sinful nature, will not inherit the Kingdom of God.

Ephesians 4:17-24. The old self (old nature, old man) is corrupt, perverse, ignorant, and hard-hearted. The new self (new nature, new man) has been re-created to be Godlike, and manifests itself in true righteousness and holiness.

DAY 5 — How Do We Use the Spirit's Gifts?

1 Corinthians 2:6-16. Paul compares the "spiritual man" with the "nonspiritual man" and explains that the nonspiritual man cannot receive the gifts of God, because they are spiritually discerned.

Romans 12:3-16. The Church is to have the proper attitude about spiritual gifts, realizing that, in the Body of Christ, we are all mutually dependent upon one another's spiritual gifts.

1 Corinthians 12:1-27. This is a description of the spiritual gifts, given by the Holy Spirit to the Body of Christ. Paul reminds them that, like parts of the physical body, each is indispensable to the welfare of the Body.

UNIT 5 What Is Not True Faith?

DAY 1 — Why Is Faith So Important?

Luke 7:1-10. Jesus was amazed at the centurion's faith. Some translations say: "Jesus marveled."

1 Peter 1:3-9. Peter said faith is more valuable than gold, because it has power for salvation of our soul.

Romans 3:21-31. Paul declared that, because we're justified by faith, there is no longer any difference between those who keep the law and those who do not keep the law.

DAY 2 — Faith Is Not Mental Assent or Acceptance of Physical Evidence

John 20:19-29. Jesus told Thomas to touch his wounds, because Thomas had said that was the only way he would believe Jesus was alive. Thomas responded by saying, "My Lord and my God."

Luke 17:11-19. The one leper returned because he saw that he was healed, and he wanted to thank Jesus. Because the other nine had not yet seen that they were healed, they kept going.

DAY 3 — Faith Is Not Works or Special Abilities

Romans 9:30-33. Paul makes it clear that faith becomes a stumbling stone for those who expect their works to gain them favor and blessings from God. This was especially true of the Jews and the keeping of the Law.

Ephesians 2:8-10. This is a clear declaration that faith is a gift of God's grace. It is not an achievement for which any man can rightfully boast.

DAY 4 — Faith Is Not Hope

1 Thessalonians 1:1-10. Paul remembered their work of faith, labor of love, and patience of hope in our Lord Jesus Christ.

1 Samuel 17. David declared that the Lord who delivered him from the lion and the bear WILL deliver him from the giant. He told Goliath with boldness that "the Lord WILL deliver you into my hand."

Psalm 23. The verbs in this Psalm are present tense, indicating David's faith in what the Lord is doing for him NOW and, therefore, will do for him "all the days" of his life, even in dark times.

DAY 5 — Faith Is Not a Feeling or a Magic Wand

Mark 10:46-52. Throwing off his beggar's rags showed that he believed he would never need them again.

Acts 8:1-25. Simon assumed that the power behind the Apostles' anointing and miracles was a result of some kind of magic.

Acts 19:11-20. They met with disastrous results. This should dispel any notion that we're to try to get anything from God through some kind of special power other than faith.

UNIT 6 What Is True Faith?

DAY 1 — Faith Is a Decision to Believe God

Deuteronomy 1:19-46. When the people of Israel heard the report from the 12 spies, they chose to believe the negative one and incurred the wrath of God and many years of wandering in the wilderness.

Deuteronomy 30:1-20. Moses told the people to choose between life and death, blessing and cursing, and their choice would affect their descendents for many generations.

Romans 4:13-21. Promises that come by faith are available to everyone who will believe. Those that come by Law are limited to those who keep the law.

DAY 2 — Faith Is a Very Real Force

Joshua 6:1-20. It was Joshua's faith and the faith of the people that led them to obey God's instructions.

1 Kings 18:20-46. In this test between the prophets of Baal and Elijah, the prophet of God, it was Elijah's faith in God that produced the awesome miracle.

Acts 3:1-16. Peter told the crowd that the miracle was done by faith in the name of Jesus.

DAY 3 — Faith Is Life

John 6:52-63. Jesus said that, as the Father gave Him life, so those who feed on Jesus will receive life through Him.

John 17:3. Eternal life is "knowing God and the Son whom he has sent."

Acts 3:15-16. Jesus is the Author of life.

DAY 4 — Faith Is a Gift from God

Ephesians 2:1-9. Paul reminds believers that even the faith with which we believe for our salvation is a gift from God.

Proverbs 3:5-8. It declares that we must trust in God with our heart and not trust our own intellect.

Romans 12:1-8. The "measure of faith" is given to believers to enable them to use their spiritual gifts for the building up of the Church.

DAY 5 — Faith Is Trusting the Word of God

Acts 14:7-10. The crippled man heard about Jesus, he believed it was true, and acted upon what he had heard and believed.

Romans 10:8-21. This scripture declares that faith comes by hearing the Word of God and choosing to believe it.

Acts 4:1-4. The people heard the Gospel preached, believed it and accepted it. From their faith, the Church was born.

UNIT 7 How Do We Use Faith?

DAY 1 — Remember Who Lives in Us

John 15:1-10. Jesus tells us to stay vitally connected to Him and the Father, like branches to a vine, if we're to keep His life in us, enabling us to bear fruit for the Kingdom.

Colossians 2:6-15. Paul reminds us to stay rooted and grounded in Jesus Christ, remembering that He has conquered all demonic powers. This will help us avoid the deceptions of false teachers.

1 John 4:1-6. He tells us to "try the spirits" to see whether they're on God's side or are opposing God. Then he tells us to remember that the Greater One lives in us, implying that, with His power, we can triumph over the enemy.

DAY 2 — Focus on the Promises, Not the Problems

Joshua 1:1-9. As Joshua was about to lead Israel into the Promised Land, God told him to be strong and of good courage. The key to his success would be to meditate on the Law day and night and to be careful to obey it.

Hebrews 5:11-14 and **6:1-3**. In order to become mature in spiritual matters, believers should constantly train their senses to distinguish good from evil and move beyond elementary teaching

Mark 4:3-20. Jesus said the cares of this life, the deceitfulness of wealth, and the desires for other things would choke out the Word and make us unfruitful.

DAY 3 — Apply the Force of Faith with Words

2 Corinthians 4:13-18. Paul is saying that, like the Psalmist (Ps. 116:10), whatever we believe strongly we will instinctively speak out.

Luke 1:35-37. The angel's announcement to the Virgin Mary declares a truth that is important for every believer: "No word from God shall be without power or impossible of fulfillment." (AMP)

Matthew 12:33-37. Jesus said our words could justify us or condemn us, for we would give account for every idle word.

DAY 4 — Be Willing to Wait as Long as it Takes

Ephesians 6:10-20. It encourages believers to take a position of authority against satanic forces, fully armed and fully trained in the Word of Truth, steadfastly refusing to back down.

Colossians 1:9-14. It is our knowledge of God and our knowledge of our place in His Kingdom that enables us to endure with patience and joy.

Hebrews 11. Some of them had such endurance and patience that they waited a lifetime without seeing their promise fulfilled.

DAY 5 — Praise God for the Victory

2 Chronicles 20:1-30. Jehoshaphat was facing an invasion by 3 united armies. In his impossible situation, he called for a fast, assembled the people to hear from God, and then sent singers ahead of his army. God gave them an overwhelming victory.

Acts 16:16-34. After being severely beaten and locked in a dungeon, Paul and Silas prayed and sang praises. God sent an earthquake and released all the prisoners. Then they led the jailer's family to the Lord.

UNIT 8 **What Are the Enemies of Faith?** Part I

DAY 1 — Insufficient Bible Study

Mark 4:11-20. Satan comes at once to steal the Word that's sown in a heart. He also uses trouble, persecution, offense, worldly worries, distractions of the age, pleasures, deceitfulness of riches, and the desire for other things.

2 Timothy 3:13-17. Depending upon the translation, this says that scripture is profitable for instruction, reproof, conviction of sin, discipline in obedience, training in righteousness, which equips us for serving God and the Church.

Hebrews 4:11-13. According to this scripture, the Word of God is quick, powerful, sharp enough to divide soul and spirit, and can discern the thoughts and intents of the heart.

DAY 2 — Prayerlessness

Acts 6:1-4. The top priorities of the early Church were prayer and the Word. It had to be their priority because they knew they must be in constant communication with God for power and wisdom to carry out His commission.

Ephesians 6:10-18. Prayer is a necessary part of spiritual warfare. Paul describes the armor we're to put on for the struggle, but prayer is the battle itself.

James 5:13-18. James gives Elijah's prayer for rain as an example of an effective, fervent prayer that God could and did answer.

DAY 3 — Pride and a Hardened Heart

Mark 7:14-23. Pride is listed here along with many other evils as something that makes us unclean.

Hebrews 3:7-19. Pride always incurs the wrath of God.

Matthew 23:1-12. Jesus equated greatness with servanthood. He said those who exalt themselves would be brought down, and those who humble themselves would be exalted.

DAY 4 — Unforgiveness and Strife

Matthew 5:21-26, 38-48. When we're treated unfairly, instead of reacting with hate and resentment, we should treat our enemy with kindness by doing more than he asked of us.

Matthew 6:9-15. If we don't forgive, God can't forgive us.

Ephesians 4:17-32. When we have an opportunity to take offense at something someone has said or done, we must learn to get over it quickly. We should respond by saying and doing only those things that we could do in the name of Jesus Christ.

DAY 5 — A Sense of Unworthiness

Ephesians 2:10. Paul says we are God's workmanship, created in Christ Jesus, to do the good works He's called us to do.

Romans 3:21-28. Paul reminds us that it is not by what we do that we find favor with God. That comes by faith in what Jesus did for us.

Galatians 3:21-29. We inherit Abraham's blessings by faith, not by keeping the Law.

UNIT 9 What Are the Enemies of Faith? Part II

DAY 1 — Double-Mindedness

Matthew 7:24-29. One house was built on rock, the other on sand. The rock represents the firm foundation of hearing Jesus' words and obeying them.

James 1:1-8. James instructed believers under trial to "count it all joy," because such experiences would produce perseverance and maturity. They were to ask God for wisdom but ask in faith, not doubting or wavering.

Psalm 112. Those who fear the Lord and delight in his commands will have a steadfast, fixed, established heart, not easily moved by bad news, because it trusts in the Lord.

DAY 2 — Greed and Covetousness

Matthew 19:16-22. The rich young ruler had to choose between following Jesus without his wealth or keeping his wealth. He chose to keep his wealth and went away sorrowing.

Luke 12:13-34. Jesus told his followers not to worry about how they were to live, but to remember how God takes care of His creatures and seek the Kingdom of God.

1 Timothy 6:6-10. Paul taught that desire for money can lead to sin and will destroy faith.

DAY 3 — Depending upon Religion or Tradition

Colossians 2:8-23. Paul taught that we should avoid anyone who teaches about any rules or traditions that are necessary for our salvation. We are complete in Jesus.

Philippians 3:3-12. Paul warned the Church to watch out for those who taught that keeping the law of circumcision was necessary for salvation.

2 Timothy 3:1-7. Paul warned that we should avoid those who come with sinful, evil hearts but with the outward appearance of godliness.

DAY 4 — Fear

Romans 8:12-16. Paul reminds us that in Jesus we are free, but if we fall back into fear, it will be like falling back into slavery.

1 John 4:16-19. This tells us that fear has to do with punishment, but God's love for us drives out fear.

Psalm 91. To receive God's promises of protection, we must remain in the shelter of the Most High. For Christians, that is in Jesus.

DAY 5 — Wrong Confession

Matthew 15:10-20. Jesus taught that evil thoughts originate in the heart of man, not from outside of him.

James 3:3-12. The tongue, like a fire, can corrupt the whole person, and it can be used for praising God or for cursing.

Deuteronomy 6:4-9. The Hebrew fathers were instructed to teach their children the laws of God all the time, whether walking or sitting. They were to bind the laws around their arms to help them remember.

UNIT 10 Where Am I Now in My Spiritual Growth?

DAY 1 — Who Is Ruling My Life?

Matthew 5:2-12. This is from Jesus' Sermon on the Mount. The Beatitudes tell of the blessings God has for those who humbly seek Him and His Kingdom.

Matthew 6:5-15. Every time we pray the Lord's Prayer we acknowledge the Kingship of God and our dependence upon Him.

Philippians 4:7-16. Paul said he had relinquished all of himself in order to know Jesus. He reminds us that our true citizenship is with Him in heaven.

DAY 2 — How Steadfast Am I in Times of Trial?

2 Timothy 3:10-14. Paul told Timothy that his own life is an example of how to face trials. He said evil will continue, but remember what you have learned and that God had always delivered him.

1 Peter 2:9-25. Peter tells sufferers to follow Jesus' example and refuse to retaliate or threaten the persecutors.

1 Peter 4:1-19. We should view trials and sufferings as tests of the strength of our faith. We should forgive our offenders and trust our soul to God.

DAY 3 — Do I Know How to Do Spiritual Warfare?

1 Peter 5:6-10. Paul tells us we should cast all our cares on Jesus, and we're to resist the devil, firm in our faith.

Ephesians 6:10-18. We are to put on the armor of God so we can take a stand against the devil's schemes.

2 Corinthians 10:1-6. The weapons of our warfare are not carnal, but they have divine power to pull down strongholds and every argument that sets itself up against the knowledge of God.

DAY 4 — Is My Life a Model of Holiness?

2 Corinthians 6:1–7:1. Paul describes his own life as a model for us. Through all the difficult trials of his life, he remained set apart from the contamination of the world.

Ephesians 4:17–5:21. Some of the practices of the "old man" are lying, anger, stealing, corrupt and evil speaking, sexual immorality, and drunkenness. Paul said we should "put them off."

Colossians 3:1-11. We can remain holy by remembering that we have been "raised with Christ." We should set our minds on higher things and consider ourselves dead to this world and hid in Christ. We are to kill the evil impulses and put on the new man, which is being renewed in God's image.

DAY 5 — Am I Abiding in Christ?

John 15:1-17. To abide in Jesus, we must remain attached to "the vine" (Jesus). The word must abide in us, we must keep His commandments and remain in His love.

Colossians 2:1-11. In Jesus, we have all wisdom and knowledge and the fullness of the Godhead. We remain built up in Him and rooted and grounded in Him. We are complete in Him.

Ephesians 3:14-21. This is a request for revelation knowedge of who we are IN Christ and all that we have when we are IN Him.

Real Problems... Real People... Real Life... Real Answers...
THE INDISPUTABLE POWER OF BIBLE STUDIES

Through the Bible in One Year
Alan B. Stringfellow • ISBN 1-56322-014-8

God's Great & Precious Promises
Connie Witter • ISBN 1-56322-063-6

Preparing for Marriage God's Way
Wayne Mack • ISBN 1-56322-019-9

Becoming the Noble Woman
Anita Young • ISBN 1-56322-020-2

Women in the Bible — Examples To Live By
Sylvia Charles • ISBN 1-56322-021-0

Pathways to Spiritual Understanding
Richard Powers • ISBN 1-56322-023-7

Christian Discipleship
Steven Collins • ISBN 1-56322-022-9

Couples in the Bible — Examples To Live By
Sylvia Charles • ISBN 1-56322-062-8

Men in the Bible — Examples To Live By
Don Charles • ISBN 1-56322-067-9

7 Steps to Bible Skills
Dorothy Hellstern • ISBN 1-56322-029-6

Great Characters of the Bible
Alan B. Stringfellow • ISBN 1-56322-046-6

Great Truths of the Bible
Alan B. Stringfellow • ISBN 1-56322-047-4

The Trust
Steve Roll • ISBN 1-56322-075-X

Because of Jesus
Connie Witter • ISBN 1-56322-077-6

The Quest
Dorothy Hellstern • ISBN 1-56322-078-4

INSPIRATIONAL STUDY JOURNALS

In His Hand
Patti Becklund • ISBN 1-56322-068-7

In Everything You Do
Sheri Stout • ISBN 1-56322-069-5

Rare & Beautiful Treasures
Nolene Niles • ISBN 1-56322-071-7

Love's Got Everything To Do With It
Rosemarie Karlebach • ISBN 1-56322-070-9

Problemas Reales... Gente Real... Vida Real... Respuestas Reales...
EL INDISCUTIBLE IMPACTO DE LOS ESTUDIOS BÍBLICOS

A través de la biblia en un año
Alan B. Stringfellow • SBN 1-56322-061-X

Preparando el matrimonio en el camino de Dios
Wayne Mack • ISBN 1-56322-066-0

Mujeres en la Biblia
Sylvia Charles • ISBN 1-56322-072-5

Parejas en la Biblia
Sylvia Charles • ISBN 1-56322-073-3

Decisión Difícil
Dr. Jesús Cruz Correa & Dra. Doris Colón Santiago •
ISBN 1-56322-074-1